ERRATA SLIP

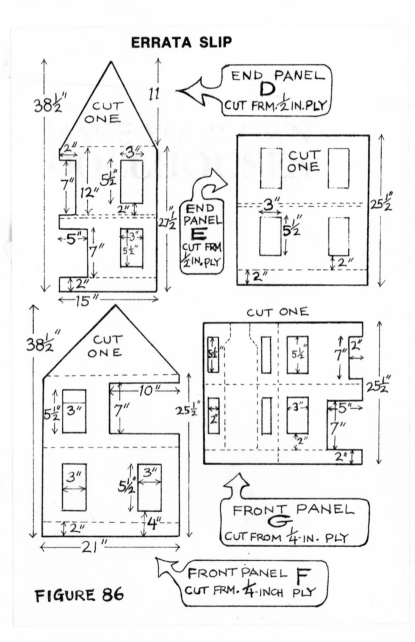

FIGURE 86

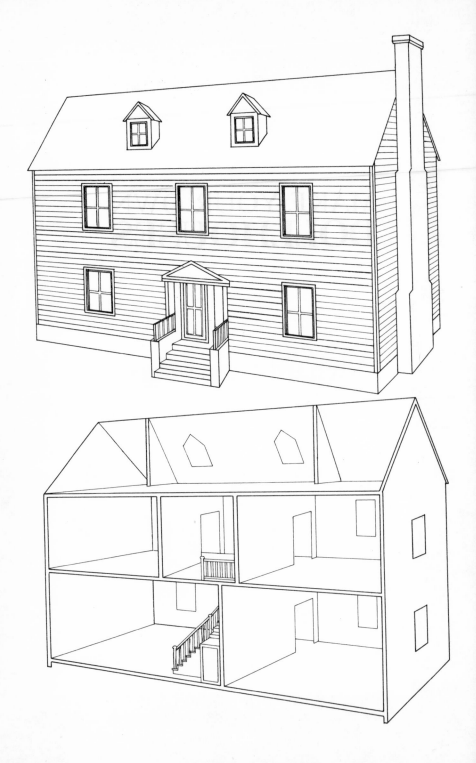

MAKE YOUR OWN
DOLLHOUSES

Written and Illustrated by
Richard Cummings

DAVID McKAY COMPANY, INC.
NEW YORK

Fig. 1: Detail from Figure 28.

Library of Congress Cataloging in Publication Data

Gardner, Richard M
    Make your own dollhouses.

    Includes index.
    SUMMARY: Instructions for building dollhouses
in various styles including a basic house, Cape Cod,
Colonial, Victorian, and an eight-unit
apartment building.
    1. Doll-houses—Juvenile literature. [1. Doll-
houses. 2. Handicraft] I. Title.
TT175.3.G37   745.59′23   77-20088
ISBN 0-679-20439-3

10 9 8 7 6 5 4 3 2 1

Manufactured in the United States of America

Book design: Helen Roberts

To John Abraham, Jack-of-all-trades, who helped build
our house and our dollhouses; and to his daughter, Anna,
my wife, who designs and brings charm and love to
the interiors of all our houses

CONTENTS

and more advanced skills. Plywood shell, open on two sides. Features plate-glass windows and operating elevator. Can be electrified.

5 VICTORIAN 124

Two stories, eight rooms and attic. Plywood shell opens at rear. Requires special tools and more advanced skills. Features tower, balcony, gingerbread woodwork.

MAKE YOUR OWN
DOLLHOUSES

WHY THIS BOOK?

Perhaps you are one of the vast number of people, both young and old, who would like to have a dollhouse of your own. You may be aware of the increasing popularity of dolls and miniature furniture on the market in all price ranges. Or you may already know the fascination and immense pleasure of miniatures.

But ready-made dollhouses are expensive, and even the do-it-yourself dollhouse kits are priced out of reach of many budgets. So we have put together this book to help you cut costs by making your own dollhouse.

The first two dollhouses described in this book can be easily constructed without help by the young people who will use them. The last three dollhouses described are more elaborate and will require more time and effort to construct. But none of the instructions and skills are beyond the capacity of the average person.

Don't be timid. Remember that what looks difficult at first never seems so difficult once it is finished. You will learn a great deal. You will earn pride in having taken matters into your own hands.

And you will have a dollhouse of your own.

WHAT'S IN THIS BOOK?

This book contains plans and instructions for making five different dollhouses, plus suggestions for making half a dozen variations of them. The five main projects are arranged so that the simplest and least expensive are in the front section of the book, the more challenging and costly in the back. The basic house can be put together in a few hours with inexpensive pasteboard. The Victorian house requires a wider range of materials and skills and may take as long as a month to complete.

Information on tools, materials, and construction techniques are scattered throughout the book and can be located in the Index and the Appendix, which includes lists of retail and mail-order suppliers, magazines, and books.

Because the Colonial is by far the most popular design for a dollhouse, and because it demands virtually all the skills of good dollhouse construction, the bulk of this book's instructional value is contained in Chapter 3.

The first two dollhouses in the book can be put together without help from Chapter 3. The two projects that complete the book require close consultation with Chapter 3. If you are interested in making the world of dollhouses more than a passing fancy, it would be helpful to read Chapter 3 before deciding which project you want to tackle. Much of the material, such as that on electrifying a dollhouse, will not seem so formidable once you have read the instructions.

1
BASIC HOUSE

Here is a dollhouse that can be made in a short time from a pasteboard box and other materials found in most homes and with a few simple tools and basic skills. We put together the shell of this six-room, two-story house in less than an hour. Painting, finishing, and decorating took a few hours more. A day's work should produce a completed home for your dolls and furniture. This chapter includes some suggestions for other pasteboard structures.

MATERIALS

You will need at least one corrugated pasteboard box in good condition. We used a box acquired from a grocery store. Liquor and hardware stores are other sources for boxes made of corrugated pasteboard and, sometimes, of wood. Our box was 8 inches deep, 16 inches long, and 12 inches wide. This is an average size. The dimensions of the original box will determine the dimensions of your house, but try to select a box that is at least 12 inches wide, since the house should be on the 1-to-12 scale.

Most dollhouses are built on the 1-to-12 scale, and most dollhouse furniture is made on the same scale. One inch in the dollhouse represents one foot in the full-sized version. In a full-

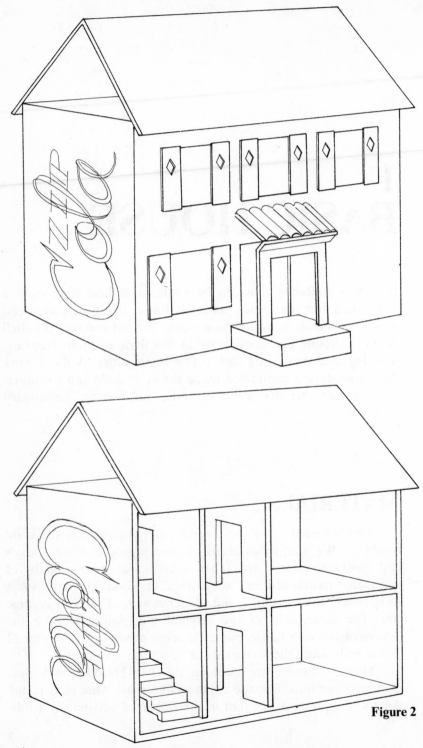

Figure 2

4

sized house there must be at least 6 feet between floor and ceiling; in a dollhouse there should be at least 6 inches. There will be two floors in your basic house. Therefore, you will need a box at least 12 inches wide.

Our box included inside sectioning to accommodate 24 bottles, and we used three of these sheets of pasteboard to make the second floor and the dividing walls. A fourth sheet was used for the porch and shutters. If your box does not include inside sectioning, cut second floor, dividers, porch, and shutters from another box.

Other materials needed for the shell are:

> White glue (or contact cement or epoxy)
> Masking tape (or decorators' tape)
> Straight pins (or designers' pins)

For exterior and inside finishing and decorating you will need:

> Poster paints (tempera) or acrylic paints, in white
or beige, and brown

Figure 3

Wrapping paper with small-figured design (or miniature wallpaper)
Plastic wrap (or sheet plastic) for windows
Fabric scraps for curtains
1 felt pen (with penetrating ink), red, green, or black

TOOLS

You will need a good cutting blade of the sort illustrated in Figure 4. X-acto offers excellent selections of craft knives with interchangeable blades, like the one shown, C. Single-edged razor blades, E, are adequate but difficult to handle because of their small size. A common utility or mat knife, D, with removable blades, is useful for cutting heavy cardboard and even light plywood.

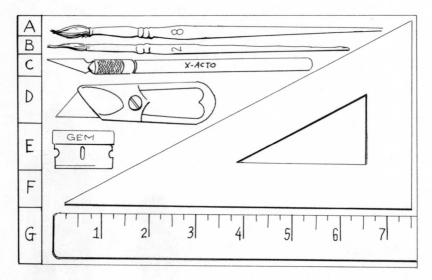

Figure 4

You will need at least one small brush for exterior and interior decorating. A No. 8 brush, A, is adequate for most purposes. Sable or camel's-hair brushes are best. A No. 2 brush, B, is helpful for finer work.

For marking cut-lines on the pasteboard, you will need a sharp No. 2 pencil and a straightedge or ruler, G. (For conversion from inches and feet to metric measurements, see the conversion table on page 146.) A triangle, F, is helpful in drawing right angles.

THE SHELL

To get an idea of the layout of the house, study the floor plan shown in Figure 5. The walls crossing the rectangles—E, C, F, and D—are known as dividing walls. They and the second-floor panel are to be inserted after the box is prepared.

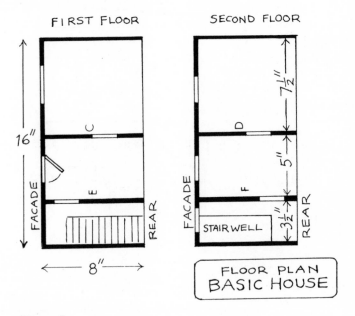

Figure 5

Remove the top of the box and stand it on its side, as indicated at the top of Figure 6. The bottom of the box will be the front or façade of your house. The top (from which the pasteboard has been removed) will become the rear of the house and will be left open to give access to the rooms on both floors.

Using your straightedge and triangle, draw the front door

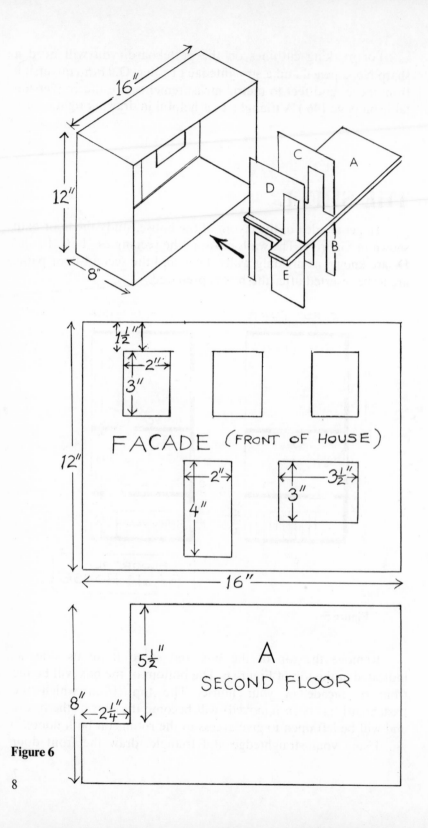

FACADE (FRONT OF HOUSE)

A
SECOND FLOOR

Figure 6

and windows on the façade in the positions and dimensions shown in the center of Figure 6. Then cut them out with your utility knife.

From a separate sheet of pasteboard, cut out the second floor, as shown in Figure 6, A; and the four dividing walls shown in Figure 7. Note that dividing walls B and C are identical. D and E have the same outside dimensions as B and C but have the doors in different locations.

Now you are ready to place the second-story floor and the room dividers. If your box already has inside sectioning, you need only remove some of the sections, leaving enough to form the second-story floor and room dividers. If you have had to cut the floor and dividers from a separate sheet, insert the second-floor panel, A, and glue it in place. Half-inch strips of pasteboard can also be cut and glued along the end walls to keep the floor more firmly in place. Otherwise, use straight pins to hold the panel in place until the glue dries. Next, insert the wall dividers and glue them in place in the positions indicated at the top of Figure 6.

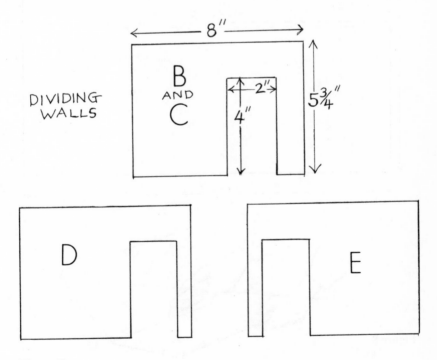

Figure 7

Half-inch strips can be added for reinforcement, or you can hold the dividers in place with straight pins.

You will notice that the edges of cut cardboard at the back of the box are open, exposing the corrugated inside of the pasteboard. These edges can be finished by folding strips of masking tape or decorators' tape along their lengths.

Make the roof from the top of the box, which has been set aside, or cut it from another sheet of pasteboard according to the dimensions shown in Figure 8. With your straightedge as a guide,

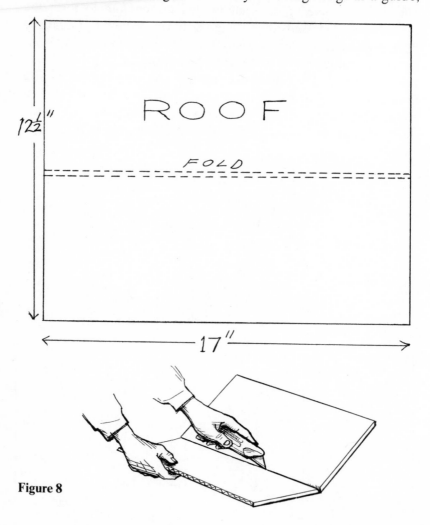

$12\frac{1}{2}''$

ROOF

FOLD

17''

Figure 8

use your knife to score a line down the length of the roof, as shown in Figure 8. If you cut only halfway through the pasteboard, you will be able to neatly bend the panel back along the scored line, creating the peak of the roof. Glue the roof into position on the top of your house, as shown in Figure 2. You may conceal the cut edges along the peak with a strip of masking or decorators' tape.

For the porch, shutters, and inside stairs, select one of the extra inside sections or cut a panel from a second box. Using straightedge and triangle, draw the porch and shutters and a strip for the stairs, as indicated in Figure 9. The porch consists of two parts: H-I and H-II. Score each along the dotted lines and bend

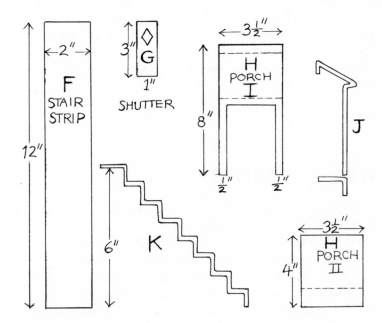

Figure 9

into the shapes indicated, J. Then glue them into place outside the main door in the positions indicated in Figure 2 at the beginning of this chapter. The boxlike shape, H-II, constitutes the body and floor of the porch. The second shape, H-I, becomes the columns and roof of the porch.

For the tile effect on the roof of the porch (see Figure 2), peel one outer paper surface from a piece of pasteboard, revealing the corrugated inside. Glue this to the roof of the porch, ridged side up.

Cut out the shutters and glue them into position on either side of each window, as indicated in Figure 2.

For the inside stairway, score the strip, Figure 9, F, at ¾-inch intervals down its length. Bend along the scored lines to form the step effect shown, Figure 9, K. Fit this into the position indicated in the floor plan, Figure 5, so that it reaches up into the stairwell opening in the second floor. Glue and hold in position with straight pins until the glue has dried.

You have completed the basic shell of your "instant" dollhouse.

BASIC FINISHING

First study these simpler and quicker methods for decorating the exterior and interior of the house:

Paint the outside with a base color such as white, off-white, or beige. Cover the leading edges of the walls and floors at the back of the house, but do not paint the interior walls. Use a water-soluble paint, as oil tends to permeate and decompose the pasteboard. Acrylic paint is best. Poster paints (tempera) will have to be applied in two or more coats in order to cover any printing on the box. If you have some interior latex paint around the house, that will do. Avoid thinning the paint too much, because a watery consistency will warp the pasteboard.

When the paint is dry, use a felt-tip pen to outline the woodwork of the doors and windows, following the patterns of the real woodwork shown in Figures 10, 19, 25, 42, and 46. If you want an effect of colored trim, use red or green instead of black. Next, using your straightedge as a guide, draw parallel lines to

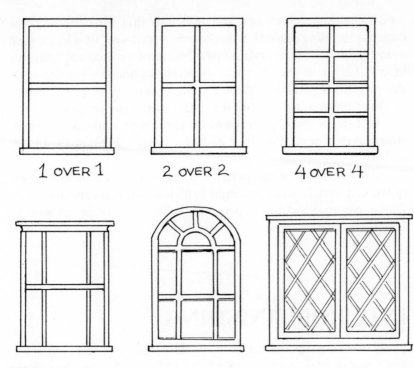

1 OVER 1   2 OVER 2   4 OVER 4

Figure 10

simulate clapboard siding, as shown in Figures 25 and 60. The shutters and porch posts can also be decorated in a harmonizing color.

WINDOWS

Windows can be glazed with plastic wrap. Cut a rectangle of film to the window size plus an extra inch all around. Pin this to a slab of pasteboard to hold it flat, then draw in the crossbars, or mullions, of the windows with your felt-tip pen, following one of the patterns in Figure 10. Finally, stretch the plastic film "glass" across the window on the inside wall and hold it down with masking or cellophane tape, or glue it with plastic cement.

If you have some pieces of thicker clear plastic, such as that used to package cosmetics and toys, cut that into the window dimensions, using scissors, a fine-toothed craft saw, or a knife with a heated blade. Cut ¼-inch strips of masking or medical adhesive tape and lay it on the outside of the windowpane in your choice of the patterns shown in Figure 10. Then mount the pane on the inside of the wall and secure it in place with tape or glue.

Cut doors from pasteboard or cardboard and mount them with hinges of tape. For door patterns, consult Figures 19, 44, 45, and 46.

Paint the roof of the porch and the roof of the house brown or red or green. If you use a light-brown paint, you can then use a felt-tip pen to draw the shapes of shingles. See Figures 26 and 59 for shingle patterns.

INTERIOR FINISHING

You can paint the inside walls white or any color you wish, and you can paper some or all of the walls. Find some decorative wrapping paper, Christmas or otherwise, and select patterns with small figures. Shopping bags are sometimes decorated in patterns small enough for miniature wallpaper, and some of the papers used in book binding are equally suitable. Using the methods shown in Figure 38, cut out a sheet of paper to fit each wall and paste it on with rubber cement or white glue.

Paint the inside stairway and the floors brown. When the floors are dry, use your straightedge and pen to draw floorboard outlines, following one of the patterns shown in Figure 22.

Curtains should be cut from the lightest material you have on hand. The easiest way to hang them is to glue them into position, using straight pins to hold them until the glue is dry. Glue them at their gathering points, at the bottom as well as along the top.

Your basic dollhouse is ready, and you may now move in the furniture and inhabitants.

FANCY FINISHING

Many other suggestions for adding interior and exterior detail are scattered throughout this book.

The outside walls can be given a three-dimensional clapboard effect by cutting miniature boards from pasteboard and gluing them in place, as shown in Figure 60. For other details, consult the Index under such listings as Shutters, Window boxes, Stairways, Brick effects, Stone effects, Tile floors, Fireplaces, Chimneys, and Fabric wall coverings.

VARIATIONS

This basic house can be modified with a few simple pasteboard additions to become one of the variations shown in Figure 11: Southern Colonial, A; farmhouse, B; or small Victorian, C.

Pasteboard can be made doubly strong by laminating two or more sheets together. Coat all inside surfaces with contact cement, allow the glue to become tacky, and then press the sheets together and hold them down with weights until the glue is dry. These laminated sheets will have sufficient strength for the creation of other house designs, such as the A-frame suggested in Figure 11, D. In fact, the two dollhouse designs that follow this one can be made from laminated pasteboard. They will not, however, be as sturdy as those made of plywood.

CAUTION: DO NOT ATTEMPT TO ELECTRIFY A PASTEBOARD DOLLHOUSE.

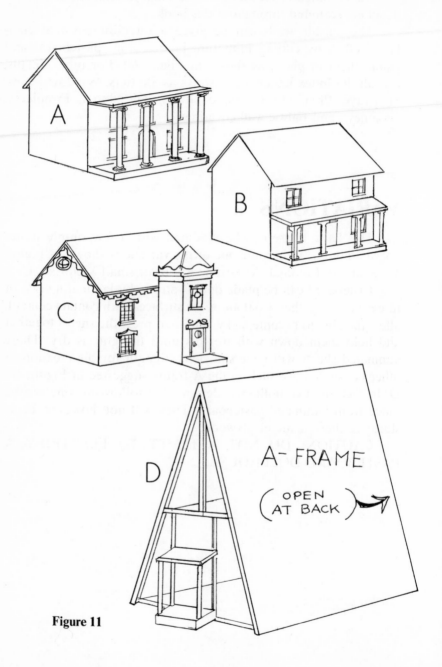

Figure 11

2
CAPE COD

The four-room Cape Cod bungalow opens at the top and front. This arrangement makes it suitable for use in a more limited play area than that required by dollhouses having access only through the rear. It also features a base that doubles as a storage box for dolls and furniture. It is made of wood and can be put together over a weekend with inexpensive materials and tools found in the average home tool box.

MATERIALS

The base, the two end walls, and the second-story floor are cut from ½-inch plywood. The roof, rear wall, and front panels are cut from ¼-inch plywood. The chimney-fireplace is cut from a 22-inch length of 2-x-4-inch pine or fir. If you decide to add the storage-box base, you will need additional ½-inch ply for the sides of the box and ¼-inch ply for the bottom.

Choosing Plywood

Plywood grades are divided into two main categories: interior and exterior. Generally, exterior is more expensive. Exterior is

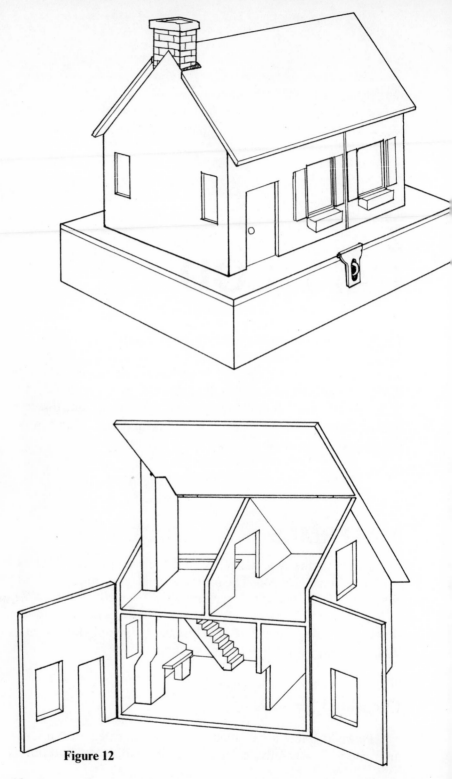

Figure 12

made with waterproof glue and should be used for all projects, indoor or outdoor, that might be exposed to excessive moisture or humidity. A-B exterior is sanded and has two good sides. It will be stamped with one or more of these grade designations: AB GI EXT EPA PSI 74. Wherever the good appearance of only one side is important, switch to A-C exterior.

Interior plywood is adequate for most dollhouse use. If you plan to paint both outside and inside walls, you will need to have both faces smooth and sound, and you should choose A-B interior (AB G4 INT APA PS 1 74). If you plan to paint only the outside walls and to cover the inside walls with wallpaper or wall fabric, choose A-D interior (AD GROUP 1 INT APA PS 74). B-B interior has two smooth sides and is inexpensive, but it has plugs, which may show through paint after a year or so.

Figure 13

The best painting surface of all is MDO, a medium-density overlaid plywood that is faced with a smooth resin-treated fiber surface heat-fused to the panel. It will be stamped with one or more of these designations: MDO BB G4 EXT APA PS 1 74. However, MDO is relatively expensive, and if you plan to glue siding onto the outside walls and paint or paper the interior walls, A-D interior is the best value. A-B interior is best if you plan to paint both sides.

Within any given category or grade there is considerable variation in quality from panel to panel. Choose sheets that have a minimum of warp and curl, so that all corners may be more easily aligned and your floors and walls will not be uneven. Take along a yardstick or a piece of lumber with a clean, straight edge, and place one of them on the face of the sheet to see if it is smooth and on an even plane. Lifting one corner and sighting along the surface of the panel will help you to find out how straight it is. All ¼-inch ply has some flexibility and will bend when lifted, but avoid any sheet that is permanently bent or curled in the extreme, especially diagonally, from opposite corner to opposite corner.

If one lumber supplier will not let you pick and choose, try another.

One 4-x-8-foot panel of ½-inch ply and one 4-x-8-foot panel of ¼-inch ply will be more than enough for this project.

Other materials needed for the shell are:

> 1 8-x-10-inch sheet of heavy cardboard
> White glue (or contact cement or epoxy)
> 1½-inch finishing nails (small heads)
> ¾-inch brads
> 6 1-inch cabinet hinges with screws
> 1 small can plastic wood

For exterior and interior finishing and decorating, you will need:

> Masking tape (or decorators' tape)
> Water-based paint (acrylic or latex)
> Walnut or maple stain
> 10 sheets No. 60 sandpaper for roofing
> Wrapping paper or miniature wallpaper
> Small strips of pine or basswood for woodwork
> Contact paper for flooring

TOOLS

You will need other tools in addition to the straightedge, utility knives, and paintbrushes required for the Basic House, page 6. A crosscut hand saw is suitable for cutting ½-inch plywood. The thinner and more delicate ¼-inch ply is best cut with a finer-toothed saw, such as a coping saw or a keyhole saw. You will also need a drill, such as a hand drill or a brace and bit, for starting inside window cuts and hinge screws. You will need a screwdriver for setting the screws. You will also need a hammer for nailing and a pair of scissors for cutting wallpaper.

If you are using power tools, your work will be easier with a circular power saw for outside cuts and an electric drill and saber saw for cutting window and door openings. An electric sander will make sanding much easier and quicker.

STEP BY STEP

Here are the steps you will be following in assembling your Cape Cod:

1. Cutting the shell parts
2. Temporary assembly
3. Covering inside walls
4. Making and hanging the doors
5. Making and installing the windows
6. Preparing the fireplace and chimney
7. Laying the floors
8. Electrification
9. Assembling the shell
10. Making and installing the stairs
11. Finishing the roof
12. Finishing the outside walls
13. Installing the flower boxes

Cutting the Shell Parts

Study the floor plan, Figure 14, to get an idea of the layout. Using straightedge and triangle, draw the various shapes on the appropriate plywood, according to the dimensions shown in Figures 15, 17, and 18. The diagrams indicate which parts are to be cut from ½-inch ply and which from ¼-inch ply. If you intend to include the storage box, draw the larger base panel, L, Figure

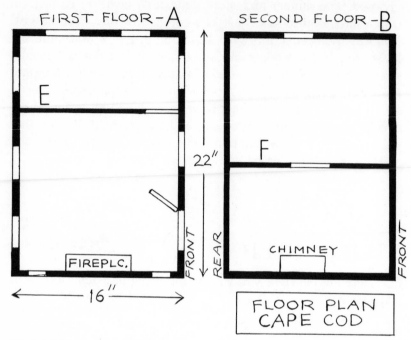

Figure 14

18, and the other parts of the box as illustrated, M and N. If you do not plan to include the storage box, cut only the base panel shown in Figure 15 as the first floor, A.

Then cut the parts. For inside cuts, such as window openings, drill holes at two diagonally opposite corners. Then insert keyhole, coping, or saber saw and complete the cut around the rectangle. Lightly sand all edges to remove splinters and rough spots.

Temporary Assembly

Temporarily assemble the parts to be sure they will fit together in the manner illustrated in Figures 16 and 19. You can tack them lightly in position with finishing nails driven in a quarter of the way. If there are any mistakes, now is the time to make adjustments, either by sanding or by recutting. Although our plan calls for merely gluing and nailing the second-floor panel (Figure 15, B) and the room dividers (Figure 17, E, F, G, H) into position, you may elect to rout grooves in the end panels, floor,

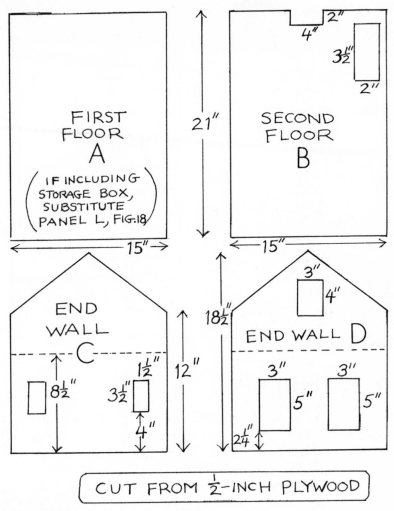

FIRST FLOOR **A**

(IF INCLUDING STORAGE BOX, SUBSTITUTE PANEL L, FIG.18)

SECOND FLOOR **B**

END WALL **C**

END WALL **D**

21″   15″   18½″   12″

CUT FROM ½-INCH PLYWOOD

Figure 15

and ceiling for a closer fit. Routing is the cutting of grooves or dados in the surface along the lines where the edge of a dividing wall meets a ceiling or floor. This usually requires a special power tool.

Once the parts are cut and sanded, the tendency is to rush ahead and assemble the shell permanently. But it is best to put in the windows and doors first and to complete the major inside details before putting the shell together, since working in the close quarters of the assembled shell is difficult.

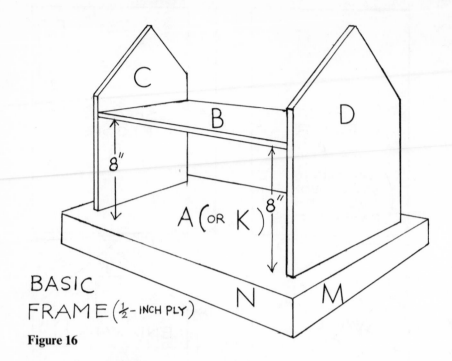

C

B

D

8"

A (or K) 8"

BASIC
FRAME (½-INCH PLY)

N

M

Figure 16

Covering Inside Walls

We chose to paint the main room of our Cape Cod and to paper the walls of the downstairs kitchen and the two upstairs rooms. But it would be easier and quicker to paint all the inside walls.

Most real wallpaper is unsuitable for dollhouses. Very few wallpapers have designs small enough for miniature effect. Many wrapping papers have small-figured designs, as do some of the papers used for binding books. Miniature wallpaper, designed especially for use in dollhouses, is available at some hobby shops and from various outlets listed in the Appendix. We used a Christmas wrapping paper with tiny geometric designs and a small-figured paper from a department store shopping bag.

Using your straightedge and triangle and a sharp pencil, lay out the dimensions on the figured paper. Choose a pattern from those shown in Figures 15 and 17. Be sure to make all the lines straight and all the corners square. Do not attempt to cut sheets that will run around all three walls. Instead, cut a sheet for each wall to be covered. (See page 61 for methods of making neat

24

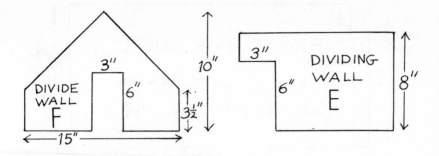

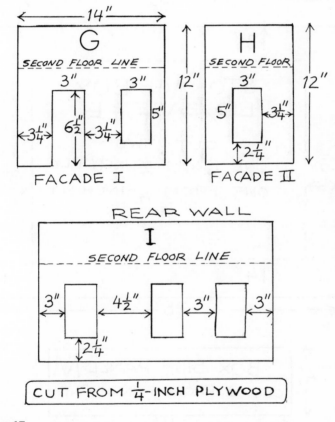

Figure 17

wallpaper corners.) Place the loose sheets in position on the unassembled wall panels and make sure your measurements are correct. If you are using a different wallpaper in each of the four rooms, the back walls will have a patchwork look until the dividing walls are in place.

You can use real wallpaper paste to hang your paper, but

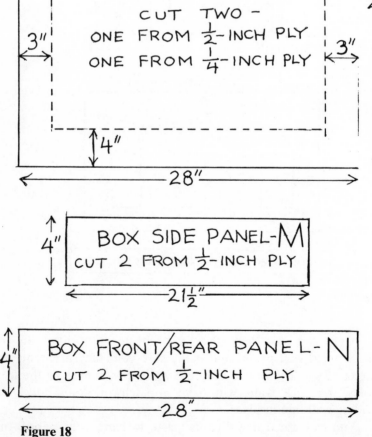

2"

1¼" FRONT ROOF PANEL J

CUT FROM ¼-INCH PLY

(ALSO REAR ROOF PANEL - K)

10¾"

23½"

3"

STORAGE BOX
LID/BASE - L

CUT TWO -
ONE FROM ½-INCH PLY
ONE FROM ¼-INCH PLY

3"

3"

22"

4"

28"

4" BOX SIDE PANEL - M
CUT 2 FROM ½-INCH PLY

21½"

4" BOX FRONT/REAR PANEL - N
CUT 2 FROM ½-INCH PLY

28"

Figure 18

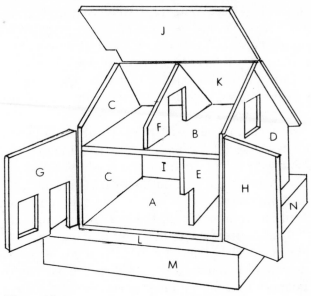

Figure 19

unless it is perfectly mixed, it will be lumpy and hard to handle. White glue is adequate, if thinned with water and brushed onto both surfaces in a very thin, even coat. Rubber cement is excellent and can also be thinned with a special solvent sold at most stationery stores. Brush a thin, even coat on both surfaces, then carefully press the paper into place. Start at one corner and smooth it toward the center, then toward the opposite corner. Paper all the walls, including both sides of each dividing wall, in this manner.

When each inside wall surface is covered, you are ready to make and mount the windows and doors, and then to frame the window and door openings.

Making and Hanging the Doors

You can make your doors from ¼-inch plywood, preferably with a veneer face of Philippine mahogany. However, basswood, because of its small and even grain, is best for all woodwork that is to be stained rather than painted. See the list of suppliers in the

Appendix for sources of basswood. Pine, of course, is more readily obtainable. Lumber yards carry pine in many sizes, and your local grocery store may have pine vegetable or fruit crates free of charge. Look for seasoned wood (not oozing sap) with a fine, straight grain. Balsawood is easy to cut and work with, but it does not stain well and will have to be covered with enamel paint.

Our Cape Cod plans call for only one operating door, the front door. But you may elect to hang movable doors in the two inside door openings as well.

A basic door can be made from a slab of ¼-inch pine or plywood, cut to the dimensions indicated in Figure 20. Lightly sand the slab with special attention to the edges. The door can be decorated with a frame of 1/16-inch strips, as indicated, A, Figure 20. Or small panels of 1/16-inch wood or good dense cardboard can be glued on, as indicated, B. Use only a minimum of glue. If the glue bulges out from under the strips or paneling, it will show through the stain. The plain door and the frame-decorated door can be stained with walnut stain, or they can be painted. The paneled door can be stained if the panels are made of wood. But if the panels are cardboard, they must be painted. More elaborate doors are available from hobby shops and dollhouse suppliers. See pages 143-145 in the Appendix.

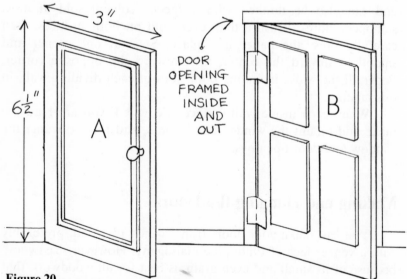

Figure 20

Doors can be hung on real hinges, but this is difficult, particularly since your wall is only ¼-inch thick. For this house we recommend hinges made of fabric, preferably a starched cambric. First glue the hinges on the inside of the door. Then mount the door and hinges in the door opening, using white glue or contact cement. Secure them with straight pins until the glue has dried. If white glue is used, a second and third coat of glue brushed over the hinges will make them stronger and more attractive.

A more complex method of hanging doors is shown in Figure 45.

Doorknobs can be cut from wood, glued in place, and painted with silver or gold paint. Small metallic beads make good knobs, as do round-headed decorator's pins, with the shaft cut off to within ⅛ inch of the head. Miniature hardware of all kinds is available from hobby or craft stores and from the suppliers listed in the Appendix.

To give both doors and windows a more finished appearance, you may want to frame them inside and out with ¼-x-1/16-inch strips of pine, basswood, or cardboard, as suggested, in Figures 21, 42, and 43.

To cut the corners of the framing more easily at 45-degree angles, you will need a miter box of the sort shown in Figure 30.

Making and Installing Windows

To construct a basic window, first make the inside frame, as shown at the top of Figure 21. This consists of two frames with the pane sandwiched between them. From lengths of 1/16-x-¼-inch or ⅛-x-¼-inch heavy cardboard, pine, or basswood, cut four patterns of side piece B and four of top-bottom piece A. From strips of 1/16-x-1/16-inch or ⅛-x-⅛-inch pine, basswood, or cardboard, cut two each of the crosspieces, or muntins, D and E.

Now assemble the two frames separately, using two A lengths and two B lengths for each. Glue them at the corners and allow to dry. Next, the pane will be cut and sandwiched between the two frames.

The pane can be made from smooth transparent film, such as plastic wrap, cut to the inside dimensions of the frame plus a 1-inch overlap. Select one of the frames and place a bead of epoxy, contact cement, or white glue around the inside surface. Allow it to dry partly, then press the sheet of film into position on one of

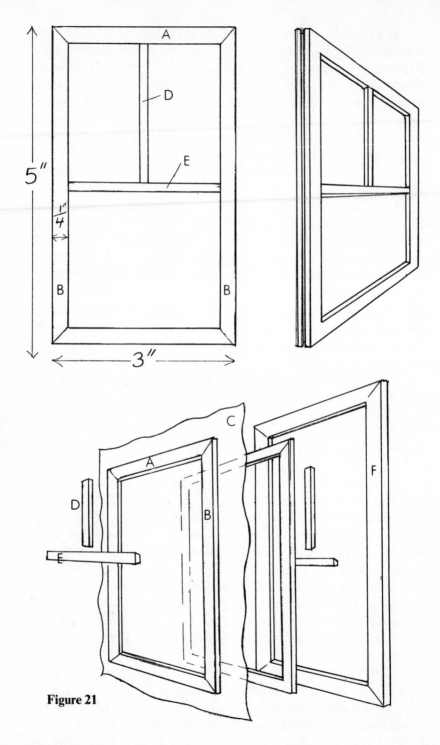

Figure 21

the frames. Add a second bead of glue on top of the film. Place the second frame on top of the first. Holding both frames of the "sandwich" together, tug gently around the protruding edges of the film to pull it taut. Secure the two frames together with straight pins, a clamp, or clothespins and allow the glue to dry thoroughly. Trim off the excess film all around.

A stiffer pane can be cut from 1/16-inch lucite, kryolite, or other clear plastic. This can be purchased at a hobby or plastics shop, or it can be cut from plastic packaging of the sort used to package cosmetics.

There is a very fine glass (1/40 inch thick) available, but it is too delicate for a dollhouse intended for active play. Glass and plastic panes can be obtained from certain of the suppliers listed in the Appendix.

Once the inside frame is glazed and assembled, add the muntins, the little dividing pieces that form the pattern of the panes, D and E. Glue two of the muntins into position on one side of the pane, the other two on the opposite side. Medical adhesive tape can also be used if you cut it to size and carefully apply it to the panes. We chose a simple two-over-one, or three-pane, pattern for our Cape Cod windows. For other patterns see Figures 10 and 42.

Try the window in its frame to make sure it fits. Correct any errors by sanding it or cutting it with your utility knife. To install, apply glue to both the edge of the frame and the edge of the window. Then press the window into place and make sure it is flush with the outside wall.

Once the window is in place, you may add the outer frame, F, bottom of Figure 21. This can be cut from 1/16-x-¼-inch pine, basswood, or cardboard. Its inside dimensions should match the outside measurements of the sandwich frame. Make two such frames for each window and glue them into position around the window on the outside and inside walls. Narrow sills, each ¼ x ½ inch, can be added to the inside and outside bottom of each window.

The making and framing of a more complex window is discussed on page 66. Window kits and ready-made windows are offered at many dollhouse outlets and can be obtained by mail from some of the suppliers listed in the Appendix.

Your windows and doors are now in place, but you are not quite ready to assemble the shell.

Preparing the Fireplace and Chimney

The fireplace and chimney are cut from a length of 2-x-4-inch pine, fir, or basswood. Select a piece of wood with a clear, straight grain and without knots. Using a handsaw and coping saw (or an electric saber saw), cut the piece in the shape and dimensions shown in Figure 22, A. Note the two extra side pieces, B, which should be cut from similar wood and glued in place, as shown. This shape is adequate as it is, but you can add a decorative frame of ¼-x-¾-inch strips around the fireplace opening. You can also add a mantel over the fireplace opening and ¼-x-½-inch strips around the top rim of the chimney, as indicated in Figure 22.

Mantel and frame can be stained or painted white, and the rest of the fireplace and chimney can be painted brick red. Or you may decide to give them a brick or stone finish.

Brick can be simulated by painting the chimney and fireplace red and outlining a brick pattern with fine white lines meant to

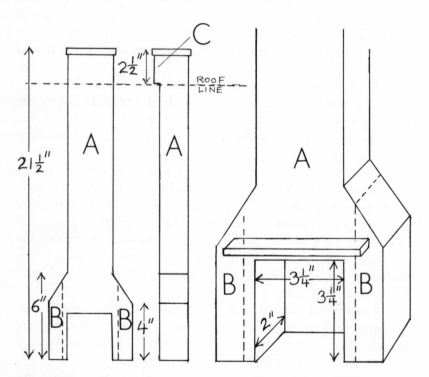

Figure 22

resemble mortar. See Figure 61 for an example. You can obtain stick-on brick patterns in both paper and relief-effect plastic from some of the mail-order outlets listed in the Appendix.

Stone effects are also available commercially. Or you may want to apply your own stone surface. One method is to cut individual stone shapes from cardboard, glue them to the surface of the chimney, paint them with stonelike colors, and fill the spaces in between the shapes with white or light-gray paint. Another method is to use one of the papier-mâché or decoupage glazes available at hobby stores. First coat the surface with a layer of glaze ⅛ to ¼ inch thick. When this is firm but not yet hard, scribe the outlines of the individual stone shapes with a pencil. (See bottom of Figure 27 for a suggested pattern.) Then paint the stones shades of gray and/or brown, and paint the scribed grooves white to simulate mortar.

You can also use real stones, held in place by one of the plastic mini-mortars available at most hobby stores. First select enough small pebbles, preferably flat on one side. Coat a small section of the chimney surface with a layer of mortar about 4-x-4 inches. The mortar dries quickly. Press the stones into place in the pattern desired, then move on to the next section. The mortar is mortar-colored and does not have to be painted.

Paint the inside of the fireplace opening with a dull (matte) black. You can also use matte black to paint a black square on top of the chimney to represent the chimney hole.

Once the fireplace-chimney is completed, glue it in position against the end wall with the small, narrow windows, as suggested in Figure 12.

Laying the Floors

It is best to finish the floors before you assemble the shell. For a quick and easy floorboard effect, paint the floors with medium-brown acrylic or latex. Allow the paint to dry. Use your straightedge and felt-tip pen or fine brush to draw one of the floorboard patterns illustrated in Figure 23. Similar floor patterns, including squares and fancy parquet, are available in stick-down sheets available at many dollhouse stores and through the mail-order outlets listed in the Appendix. Tile and linoleum floor effects are also available. Real miniature floorboards which can be

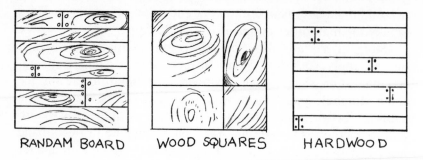

RANDAM BOARD   WOOD SQUARES   HARDWOOD

Figure 23

glued down individually or in panels, are also available. (See the Appendix.) Various kinds of contact papers, sold in most hardware and houseware stores, offer a good woodgrain effect. Get as fine and "miniature" a grain as you can.

Electrification

This house can be electrified for detailed lighting or display lighting. See page 82 for details.

Assembling the Shell

First assemble the thicker ½-inch plywood parts into the basic frame shown in Figure 16. If you are including the storage box, use the larger base panel, L, Figure 18. To prepare each piece, spread glue evenly along both edges to be joined and allow the glue to dry: three minutes for white glue, fifteen minutes for contact cement. Press the edges of the pieces together, then drive 1½-inch finishing nails into them, one nail every 3 inches and smooth it with a spatula or your finger. Instead of nails, you can use wood screws, but be sure to first drill holes to half the depth of the screw, using a bit with a diameter slightly smaller than that of the screw shaft.

If you are including the storage box, glue and nail the larger base to the ½-inch ply frame shown in Figure 25, M, N.

Now that the frame of the ½-inch panels is assembled, add the ¼-inch pieces. For these, use the same glue and ¾-inch brads.

It is best not to try to countersink the brads, but make sure you drive them firmly against the surface. First secure the rear wall, I, Figure 17. If you are adding the storage box, secure the bottom panel, O, Figure 25, which is the same size as L, Figure 18.

Next, insert the dividing walls, F and E, in the positions shown in Figure 19. First, place a bead of glue along the floor line and ceiling where the edge of the panel will rest. Add glue to the appropriate edges of the panel. Allow the glue to dry partly, then slide the panel into place. If you are using contact cement, take particular care to work deliberately, because the cement holds fast once the two surfaces make contact. Use a knife point or a screwdriver to scrape away any excess glue before it hardens.

Although the divider panels will not be nailed, you can use brads, pins, or masking tape to hold the panels temporarily in place until the glue sets.

Next, select the rear roof panel. It is the same size as the front roof panel, J, in Figure 18, except that it has the chimney notch in an opposite corner, as indicated by the dotted lines in the lower left of the diagram. Glue and nail it in the position shown, K in Figure 19.

Now it is time to hinge the front roof panel, J, and the two front, or façade panels, G and H. The hinges should have very small screws that will not completely pierce the ¼-inch ply. If the screws do penetrate, file off the protruding points. To firmly secure the hinges, apply epoxy cement between the wood and hinges before turning the screws. Epoxy is excellent for bonding materials of differing porousness—wood to plastic, metal to wood, etc. Use the same method for both front wall panels and the roof panel.

The basic shell is assembled. Before you add the exterior details, the interior needs a final addition: the stairway.

Making and Installing the Stairs

A set of basic stairs can be cut from a single piece of straight-grained pine, fir, or basswood, in the dimensions shown in Figure 24. The grain of the wood should run lengthwise up the stairs. (For a more authentic, but more difficult, stairway, see page 73.) If you wish, you can add treads of fine-grained pine or basswood. See page 76. If you add treads, they can be stained. The rest of the

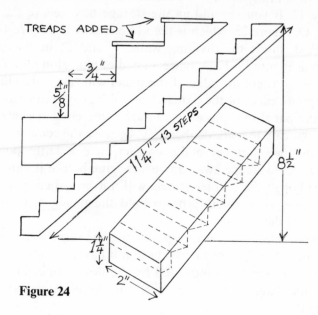

TREADS ADDED

$\frac{3}{4}''$

$\frac{5}{8}''$

$11\frac{1}{4}'' - 13$ STEPS

$8\frac{1}{2}''$

$1\frac{1}{4}''$

$2''$

Figure 24

stairway can be painted. Or you can paint the entire stairway. Handrails can be added. See page 76.

Position the stairway as indicated in Figure 12. Glue it at the bottom, top, and along the edge which goes against the rear wall.

Finishing the Roof

The roof can be painted. The most common roof colors are brown, green, maroon, red, and blue. Perhaps you will want to match your roof color to the trim color of your window frames and window boxes.

We chose to cover our roof with imitation asphalt shingles cut from No. 60 sandpaper. Cut the shingle courses in the shape and dimensions shown in Figure 26. Stick them to the roof with white glue or contact cement. Apply the adhesive to the top edge of each course and also to the lower corners of each, to prevent the corners from curling with age. Glue the courses to the roof with the sandy side up. Start at the top edge, or ridge, of the roof and work down one slope, overlapping the courses as shown in Figure

26. Do one row at a time. Then start again on the far side of the ridge and work down the opposite slope. Once the glue has dried and you are sure all the corners are glued down, you can paint the shingles the color of your choice. Acrylic paint is best, but latex will do.

Other roof coverings are discussed on page 94.

Finishing the Outside Walls

We chose to sand and then paint the outside walls of our dollhouse. White is the most common exterior house color; the more muted pastels and earth colors are next in popularity. Acrylic paints are best, but expensive for covering such a large surface. If you have some extra latex wall paint around the house, use that. If you paint with tempera, remember that it powders and smudges and should be "fixed" with an acrylic spray of the sort available in most paint and art supply stores.

The outside walls can be covered with a variety of materials, such as stone, brick, clapboard siding, or shingles. Consult the Index under those headings.

Once the walls are painted or covered with other material, you may want to paint on details, such as window and door frames, in a second color.

If you wish to add shutters, see the Index.

Installing the Flower Boxes

The two small flower boxes are made from ¼-inch plywood or, better yet, ⅛-inch pine or basswood, cut to the dimensions shown in Figure 26, P, Q. First sand the pieces and then glue them together with white glue or contact cement. Paint the boxes white or your trim color. For soil in the boxes, we used a dark shade of cork, but you could use brown-painted styrofoam or real dirt. Make small artificial flowers with crepe paper twisted onto lengths of light wire. Or you can buy miniature flowers, dried grasses, or artificial blooms, available at many gift and florist shops. Or they can be ordered from one of the mail-order outlets listed in the Appendix.

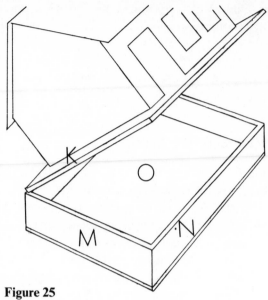

Figure 25

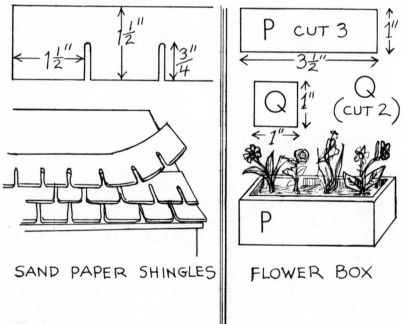

SAND PAPER SHINGLES

FLOWER BOX

Figure 26

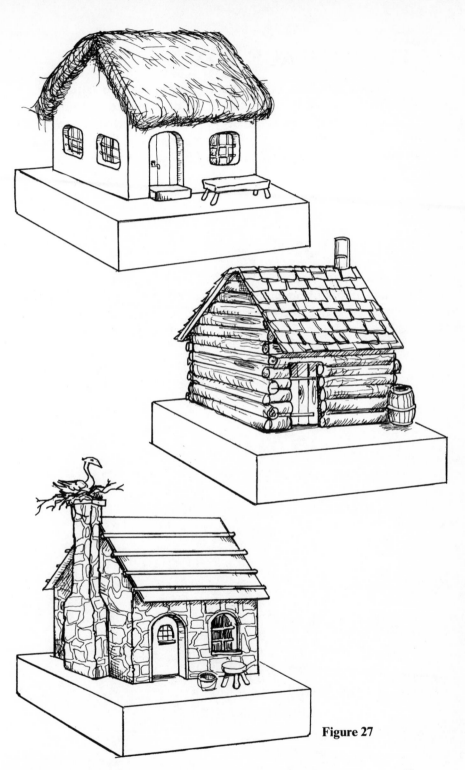

Figure 27

39

THE STORAGE BOX

If you have decided to build your Cape Cod cottage on a base that is also a box for the storage of furniture and dolls, you can now paint the base with acrylic or latex paint. The top of the box should be hinged so that when it opens, it raises the whole house at the same time, as indicated in Figure 25.

VARIATIONS

The Cape Cod shell can be altered by judicious cutting of window and door openings and by altering the exterior details to represent a thatched cottage, a log cabin, or the stone cottage of a Balkan peasant family, complete with stork. See Figure 27.

3
COLONIAL

Here is the classic American house, with five large rooms and a large attic. The Colonial design makes a good dollhouse for the same reasons it makes a good residence. It offers the maximum floor space that can be contained under one roof; its dormers are relatively simple and inexpensive to construct and give a needed touch of grace to the structure. The dollhouse is constructed of plywood and pine with some purchased basswood and cedar details. Its outside walls can be painted or covered with your choice of exterior siding: clapboard, shingle, brick, or stone. It can be electrified for display or completely wired to take a full complement of lights. Variations on this basic form appear at the end of this chapter.

This is a challenging project, requiring some special tools and purchased materials. It cannot be completed in a short time. It took over a hundred hours of work for us to complete our Colonial. But they were absorbing and ultimately rewarding hours. You may find, as we did, that your family or friends will quickly become involved in the project. There is something to do for everybody, from basic carpentry and painting to fine detail, furnishing, and decorating.

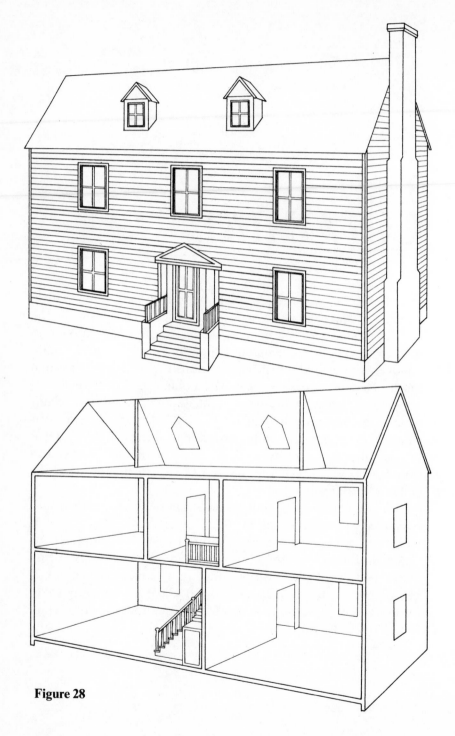

Figure 28

42

STEP BY STEP

Here is a list of the basic steps in the creation of your Colonial. Tedious as it may seem, it is worth your while to read through the list at least twice in order to acquaint yourself with the detailed instructions that follow. The order in which things are done is important in all construction; if you follow this list as you work, you can save yourself much grief. For instance, if the preliminary electrical wiring (Step 7) is not done before the floors and ceilings are covered, you will have difficulty hiding the wires.

1. Pricing
2. Gathering the materials and tools
3. Laying out and cutting parts for the shell
4. Routing for the dividing walls
5. Temporary assembly
6. Inside wall covering
7. Concealing the preliminary wiring
8. Laying the flooring
9. Making and installing the windows
10. Making and hanging the doors
11. Building the main stairway
12. Building the attic stairway
13. Building and installing the fireplace
14. Assembling the shell
15. Completing the wiring system and components
16. Installing the stairways
17. Building and installing the dormers
18. Installing the roof
19. Building and installing the chimney
20. Finishing the roof
21. Applying siding to the outside walls
22. Painting
23. Finishing the foundation
24. Making and installing the shutters
25. Building the front porch and steps
26. Final details

As you read through the detailed instructions, you will encounter one "skip-step" in the process. Before you can conceal the preliminary wiring (Step 7), you will have to skip ahead to Step 15 and complete the wiring system in order to decide whether you want to wire the house for display lighting or for a more extensive system. There are page cues within the text to help you make this jump forward and then back.

Pricing

You will not be able to arrive at a total cost without first reading through this entire chapter, since we offer various cost alternatives as we go along. But those decisions are the first you should make before actually starting work. Some costs, such as the price of plywood, cannot be avoided. But in other cases, such as windows and doors, you have the choice of making the items yourself, building them from kits, or buying them ready-made. Expenses can mount with surprising speed, as any builder of a real house knows. Before starting work, it is best to make a careful check of store and mail-order prices. Many items are cheaper if ordered direct from the supplier. On the other hand, the staffs of the better dollhouse and craft stores can offer encouragement and advice that may save you trouble, time, and money.

Figure 29

Gathering the Materials and Tools

MATERIALS

The shell is made from ¼-inch and ½-inch plywood. One 8-x-4-foot sheet of each will be enough. See pages 17-20 for instructions on selecting plywood. Below is a list of the other materials used to build the Colonial shown in the photograph. It should be kept in mind that this list is not fixed because of various alternatives. Once you have read through this chapter and made your decisions, you will be able to make up a more specific list of your own.

Lumber

1	4-x-8 sheet of ½-inch ply, both surfaces sanded and clear
1	4-x-8 foot sheet of ¼-inch ply, veneered on one surface with Philippine mahogany
11	pieces of miniature clapboard siding, 3½-x-48 inches (equivalent of 2,690 inches of miniature clapboards)
260	inches of ¼-inch basswood miniature molding
244	inches of basswood lumber, ½ x 3/16 inch
140	inches of basswood lumber, ¾ x ¼ inch
80	inches of basswood strip, 1/16 x 1/16 inch
70	inches of basswood strip, ¼ x ¼ inch
21	inches of basswood lumber, ⅜ x ⅜ inch
70	inches of basswood lumber, ⅝ x 1/16 inch
70	inches of oak lumber, ¾ x 1/16 inch
3	sheets of pine, fir, or basswood lumber, 5 x 12 x ¼ inch
30	inches of precut stair rail
1	package miniature teak flooring (enough to cover 1 square foot)
10	packages cedar shingles (enough to cover 6½ square feet)
4	15-inch lengths of precut stair risers
10	1-inch lengths of 1/16-inch hardwood dowling or bamboo shish kebob skewer

Assorted scraps of pine, fir, basswood, and plywood

Hardware

2   dozen four-penny, 1½-inch wire or finishing nails
1   box 1-inch, 18-gauge wire nails
12 1¼-inch machine or wood screws with flat heads
1   package straight pins, preferably round-headed decorators' pins
5   miniature brass door knobs
1   miniature brass door knob with plate
1   miniature brass door knocker

Wiring

1   12-volt transformer
1   fuse holder and fuse to take 16 volts, rated at 1500 milliamperes
15 feet small-gauge dollhouse wire, insulated and stranded
4   12-volt lumette light sockets and lumette bulbs
1   roll fine electrician's tape
2   ½-inch plastic drinking straws

Glue

2   16-ounce containers white glue (Elmer's or Sobo)
1   3-ounce container contact cement (add 1 pint if using to glue roof shingles)
1   2-tube package epoxy
1   tube or small can plastic wood

Paint

12 1-ounce bottles (or equivalent) white acrylic (TACC or other); or 1 quart white latex interior wall paint, matte finish
2   1-ounce bottles acrylic trim color of your choice (TACC or other)
1   6-ounce can mahogany or maple stain (or X-acto House of Furniture Finishing Kit)

Other

7   6-x-6-inch panels of miniature brick (Doreen Sinnett or other; see Appendix)

1   small can paste wax (or wax-base furniture polish)
9   3-x-5-inch sheets clear plastic: lucite, or other (or micro-glass; see Appendix)
2   1-x-4-inch sheets colored plastic sheeting (or micro-glass), amber or a color of your choice
4   X-acto do-it-yourself door kits for 3-x-6⅝-inch panel doors
Sandpaper
Fabric or paper for interior wall coverings (total of 2,760 square inches)

TOOLS

You will need the same tools required for the Cape Cod house: utility and craft knives, straightedge and triangle, pencil and paintbrushes, hammer, screwdriver, saws and drills. A crosscut hand saw and coping saw will do, but electric saws will be a great help: a circular saw for outside cuts and a saber saw for cutting window and door openings. X-acto makes an excellent set of knives, which includes small craft saw blades for fine cutting. Hand drills are sufficient, but an electric drill will make your work easier, as will an electric sander.

You will need a small 60-watt soldering iron for soldering the connections of the lighting system.

We used an additional special piece of equipment for cutting grooves in the floor and ceiling for the wiring conduit and the dividing walls. It was an electric router.

A miter box is helpful for cutting 45-degree angles. Purchase one at a hardware or craft store, or make your own from wood, as shown in Figure 30.

Should you decide to have more elaborate interior woodwork than ours—particularly if you intend to make your own newels, molding, and furniture—you will need one of the power tool sets made especially for craft work. The Dremel Company offers a variety of such tools, as does American Eddelstaal. Both companies will send brochures and are listed in the Appendix.

Finally, two of the handiest tools for miniature work are to be found around the average home: toothpicks for applying glue in hard-to-reach places, and cotton swabs for cleaning windowpanes and brushing sawdust out of cracks and corners.

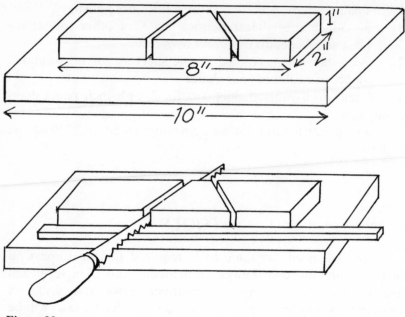

Figure 30

Laying Out and Cutting Parts for the Shell

Study the floor plans in Figures 31, 32, and 33 to get an idea of the general layout. These floor plans will serve as helpful cross references for other diagrams.

The main walls, floor panels, and dividing walls (shown in Figures 34 through 37) must be laid out and cut very carefully. A ½-inch variation in line can disturb the ultimate balance of the whole structure. Once such an error is built in, you must live with it. It is best to concentrate on the initial laying out and cutting.

"Check all measurements at least three times" is an old carpenter's maxim, and a good one.

Use a straightedge, a triangle, and a sharp pencil to draw out the parts according to the dimensions indicated in Figures 34, 35, 36, and 37. Pay close attention to the labels that indicate whether a part is to be cut from ½-inch or ¼-inch ply. If you plan to rout the floors and ceilings to receive the dividing walls, you will have to cut those dividing walls (F, G, H, I, and J) ¼ inch higher than shown in Figure 37. Also, before cutting the attic stairwell in the attic floor panel, C, Figure 35, consult page 77. If you decide to

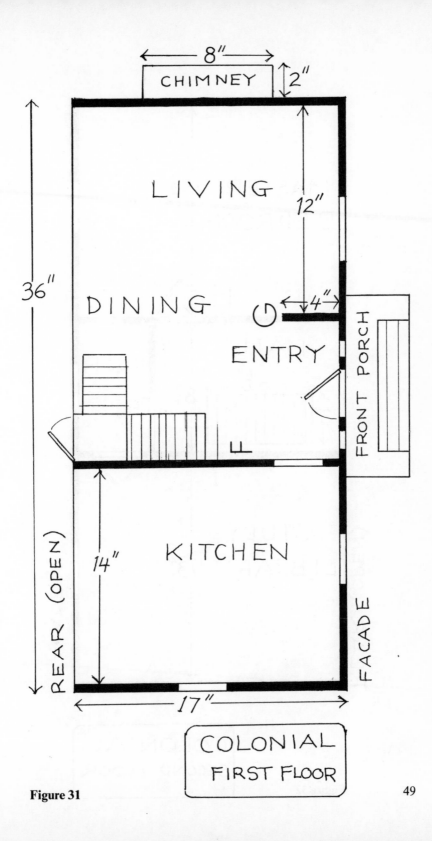

8"

CHIMNEY

2"

LIVING

12"

36"

DINING

4"

ENTRY

FRONT PORCH

REAR (OPEN)

14"

KITCHEN

FACADE

17"

COLONIAL
FIRST FLOOR

Figure 31

49

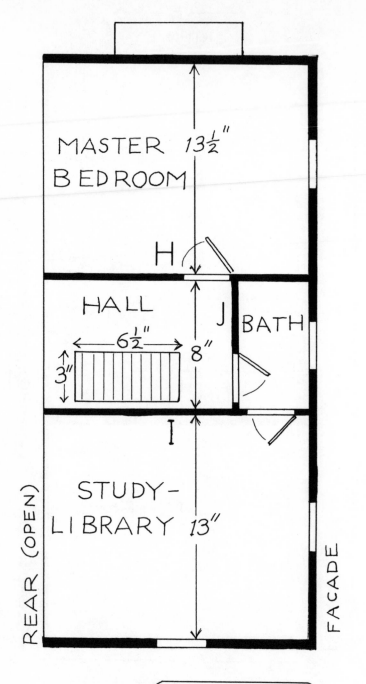

MASTER $13\frac{1}{2}''$
BEDROOM

H

HALL

$6\frac{1}{2}''$

$3''$

J

BATH

$8''$

I

STUDY-
LIBRARY $13''$

REAR (OPEN)

FACADE

COLONIAL
SECOND FLOOR

50   **Figure 32**

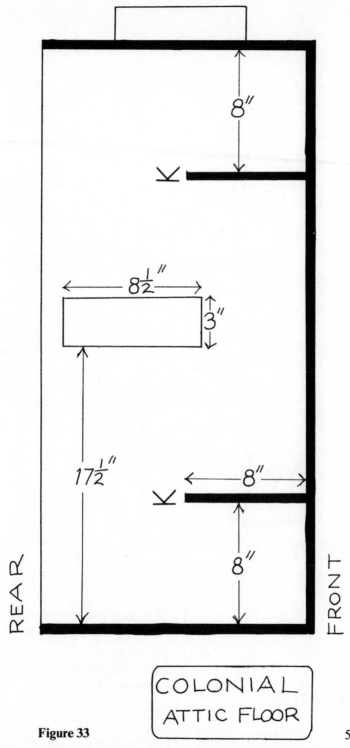

REAR

FRONT

8″

K

8½″

3″

17½″

8″

K

8″

COLONIAL
ATTIC FLOOR

Figure 33

51

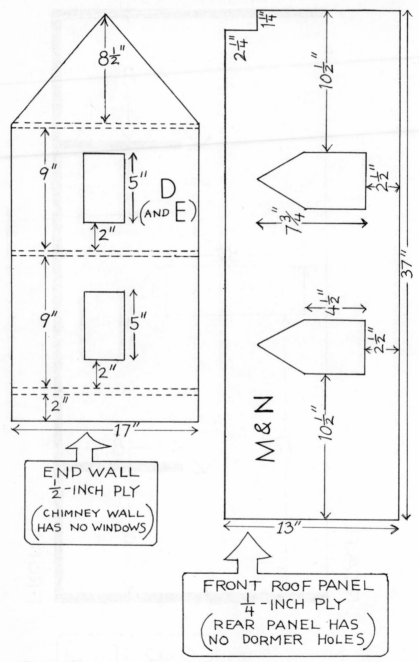

$8\frac{1}{2}''$

$9''$

$5''$

D
(AND E)

$2''$

$9''$

$5''$

$2''$

$2''$

17''

END WALL
$\frac{1}{2}$-INCH PLY
(CHIMNEY WALL
HAS NO WINDOWS)

$2\frac{1}{4}''$ $\frac{1}{4}''$

$10\frac{1}{2}''$

$2\frac{1}{2}''$

$7\frac{3}{4}''$

$4\frac{1}{2}''$

$2\frac{1}{2}''$

M & N

$10\frac{1}{2}''$

13''

FRONT ROOF PANEL
$\frac{1}{4}$-INCH PLY
(REAR PANEL HAS
NO DORMER HOLES)

37''

Figure 34

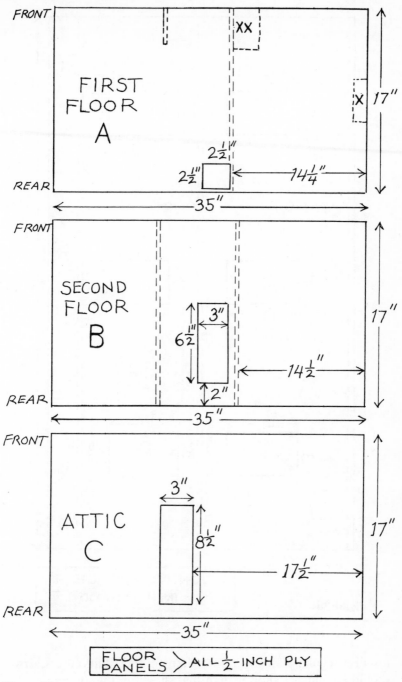

Figure 35

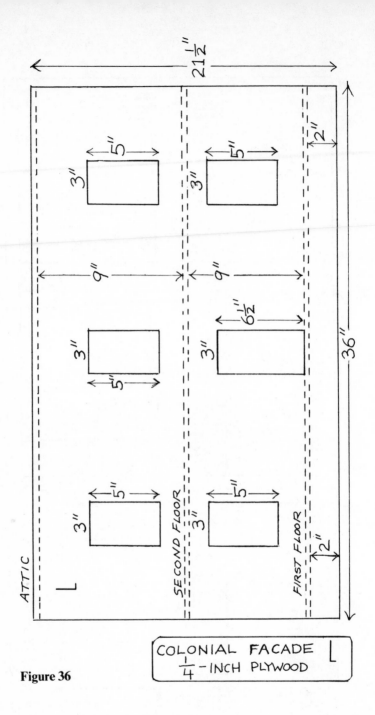

Figure 36

COLONIAL FACADE
$\frac{1}{4}$-INCH PLYWOOD

install a regular stairway rather than folding stairs, the stairwell should be 3 inches shorter than that shown in the diagram.

Once you have cut the parts, use a pencil to draw lines indicating the first, second, and third floor levels on both sides of

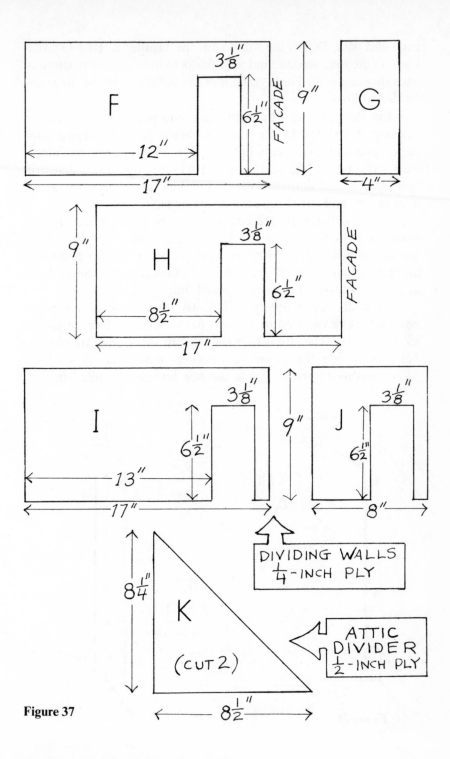

Figure 37

each end wall, D. Do the same with the façade, L. Draw similar lines on the first, second, and attic floors to indicate the position of each dividing wall. These guidelines are indicated in the diagrams by dotted lines.

Cut the parts with the same care and precision you used in drawing them. Try to run the saw blade precisely down each pencil line so that it "eats up" the line. First cut the outside of each part. To cut the stairwells and window openings, first drill holes *within* each corner of the shape, then insert a coping saw or a saber saw and cut along each inside edge.

Once all the parts are cut, select those with similar dimensions—such as the end walls, the divider walls, the three floor panels, and the attic triangles—and place them alongside one another to make sure they match on the crucial edges. Sand down any excess outside the original pencil line.

Sand all edges lightly but firmly. Wrap loose sandpaper around a block of wood to assure a flat sanding surface, or use an electric sander. The aim is to make the cuts clean and straight. Do not sand inside the proper dimensions more than 1/16 inch. Minor wavers or breaks inside the saw line can be filled in with

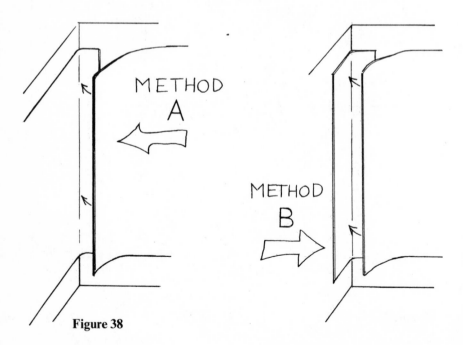

METHOD A

METHOD B

Figure 38

plastic wood later, but be sure the general outside edges are correct. If you have not correctly cut inside the pencil line, recut the piece.

Routing for the Dividing Walls

Dado joints make the structure stronger, but the purpose here is to make it possible to install the divider walls without gluing them in place. Thus, they may be slid in or out at your convenience whenever you wish to redecorate, change a wall covering, and so forth. As already mentioned, if you plan to rout floors and ceilings to receive your dividing walls, each dividing wall should be ¼ inch higher than shown in the diagrams.

Routing can be done with a handsaw and chisel, but it is difficult and hardly worth the labor. We used an electric router. Each groove should be ¼ inch wide, to accommodate the ¾-inch-thick divider wall edge, and ⅛ inch deep. You may have to use a

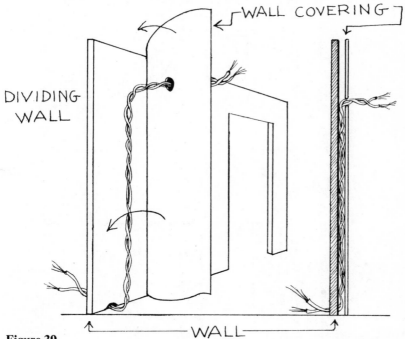

Figure 39

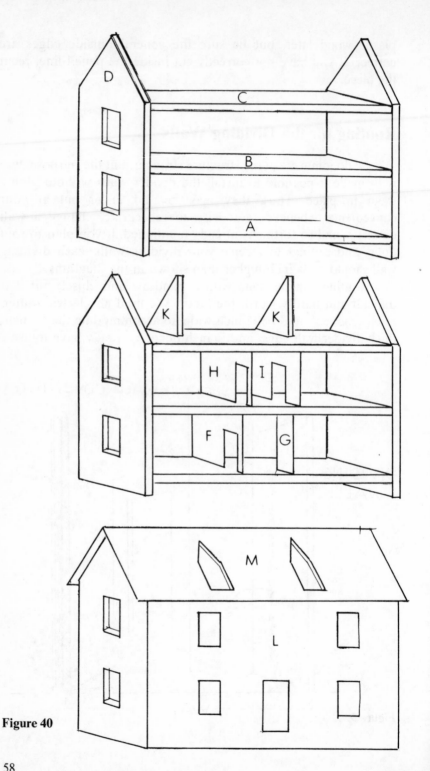

Figure 40

utility knife to slightly bevel or taper each wall edge so that it will slide in and out of the routed grooves more easily. A film of paste wax on the edges will help the walls to slide smoothly.

A router can also be used to cut grooves in the second floor to receive the electric wiring conduit (see page 63).

Temporary Assembly

Now temporarily assemble the frame of the shell, as shown at the top of Figure 40. Tack it together with 1½-inch wire nails, and drive the nails in just deep enough to hold the pieces in place. You will probably need the help of another pair of hands to hold the floor panels in position.

Next, tack the façade in place, as shown, L, bottom of Figure 40. Use 1-inch brads and drive them only halfway into the façade. Place the divider panels—F, G, H, and I—in position to make sure they fit snugly but not so snugly that the floors squeeze them and cause them to bow. Also place the attic dividers, K, and the roof panels, M and N, in position.

Locate and mark any errors, then carefully remove the nails in the order in which you placed them. Completely disassemble the shell. Correct whatever errors you can.

At this point, there is a great temptation to put on the glue and hammer the shell together permanently, but that would be a costly move. There is much still to do.

Inside Wall Covering

Wiring to be hidden under the wall coverings must be installed before the coverings can be glued on. Our wiring system consists of only four lights and is meant more for display than for realism. If you are interested in including a more complete set of lights, you should now skip ahead to pages 82–92. For a more complex system, many more wires will have to be hidden.

For our display system, three sets of wires need to be hidden under wall coverings. Consult Figures 41, 53, and 55 for a more complete picture of the system. One set of parallel wires goes on the inside divider wall of the upstairs guestroom-study, as indicated in Figure 41. The other set goes on the inside divider

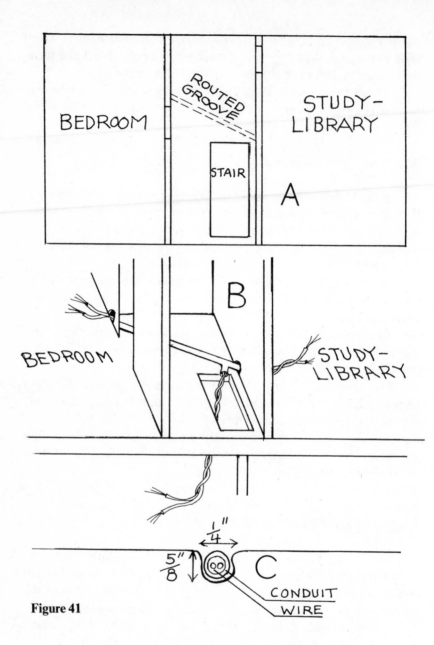

Figure 41

wall of the upstairs master bedroom. Each set consists of two wires, each wire cut to a 20-inch length. The set for the master bedroom is extended vertically upward along the wall to the point where the light fixture will be, leaving an extra 3 inches for use when the fixture is wired in. The wires are glued to the bare wall surface with contact cement, and the remaining wires at the bottom are allowed to extend loosely. They will be connected to the system later on. The set for the guestroom-study is handled in the same way. The wall coverings will then be applied over the wall surface, concealing the wires, as indicated in Figure 39.

As mentioned, if you decide to install a more elaborate system, wires may have to be hidden under the coverings of other walls.

The variety of possibilities for wall coverings is the same as that for a full-sized house. You can paint the inside walls (make sure you have the smoothest side of the plywood turned inside). If you paint, use a matte acrylic or latex. Glossy oil paint does not give a good effect in miniature because the glazed surface does not reduce to scale and seems too thick or deep.

You can hang wallpaper or fabric and add wood paneling, contact paper, or vinyl for a brick or stone effect. You can even plaster the walls by first laying on a sheet of fine wire mesh to hold the plaster.

We did one room of our house, the guestroom-study, in miniature wallpaper purchased from one of the suppliers listed in the Appendix. All the rest of our walls and ceilings were done in fabric: white cotton muslin for the ceilings and hallway walls, and various small-figured fabrics for the other rooms. The muslin gives an effective impression of smooth plastering. Fabric offers a convincing texture in miniature, provided you choose materials with tight weaves. Printed fabrics should have small-figured patterns. Glue may stain the lighter fabrics. Some contact cement dries a vivid yellow, so white glue is best for mounting fabric wall coverings. Always test the chosen fabric by first gluing a small swatch to a piece of scrap wood.

Before cutting wall fabric or paper, consider the matter of corners.

WALLCOVER CORNERS

There are two methods for achieving neat, closed corners in a papered or fabric-covered room.

For Method A, cut each panel ½ inch long at one end. This extra overhang is then creased, as shown in Figure 38, bent around the corner, and extended ½ inch onto the adjoining wall.

The edge of the next sheet can then be glued over this extra fold and butted into the corner, as shown, Method A, Figure 38.

For Method B, cut a 1-inch strip and first glue it into the corner. Then apply the two adjoining sheets. Butt them together over the strip, thus making a closed seam.

However, both methods make it impossible to do all the wall covering before assembling the shell. Both must be employed after assembly, a process that is difficult within the tight confines of the rooms.

We chose, instead, to rely on the accuracy of our original saw cuts and sanding to provide a tight fit at each inside corner. Each panel of wall covering was cut to fit exactly against each floor, ceiling, or wall line. These join lines were successfully covered by the butt ends of adjoining floors, ceilings, and walls.

Obviously, use of Methods A and B will also make it impossible to slide divider walls in and out from their routed grooves.

CUTTING AND GLUING WALL COVERING

For our method, cut out a panel of wall covering for each wall surface, following the dimensions shown for each wall and ceiling in Figures 34 through 37. These dimensions can tolerate an outside overlap, or variation, of ¼ inch for the ½-inch surfaces and ⅛ inch for the ¼-inch surfaces, since the variations will be covered when the shell is assembled. There is also some tolerance in window openings and doorways, since the window and door framing will cover the edges. We bent the paper or fabric over all those leading edges that would show at the rear of the dollhouse, since they would be covered later with wood strips.

To glue down the wall coverings, use rubber cement for paper, white glue for fabric. Spread either of them in very thin and even layers on the wall surface. Pay special attention to the outer edges. In the case of paper, apply an equally thin coat to the back of the paper. Press the panel carefully into position, making sure every inch of the surface makes smooth contact with the glue. Smooth out all air bubbles. When smoothing the fabric, be careful that you do not pull the design awry.

Allow the glue to dry, then examine the edges for any raveling or tufts that have not stayed down. Apply touches of glue and press the tufts flat.

Cover all inside walls in this manner, including the inside surfaces of the roof panels and the triangular attic dividers. The inside walls, particularly the inside of the façade wall, will now look something like patchwork, but they will quickly become the walls of individual rooms when the shell is finally assembled.

Concealing the Preliminary Wiring

More wiring must be installed before the floors are covered. For a more complex system, wires may also be hidden under the ceiling covering. For our system, wiring is hidden only under wall covering and under the hallway flooring.

Rout two grooves or channels in the plywood floor surface, as shown in Figure 41. These routed grooves should be ½ inch wide by 5/16 inch deep. (If you plan to slide the dividing walls in and out, you will have to try to cut the grooves 1/16 inch deeper at those points where the conduit will pass under the wall.)

The channels can be cut with an electric router or with a saw or utility knife. Next, install two lengths of conduit cut from lengths of ¼-inch plastic drinking straw. The two lengths of conduit are then glued into the channels with contact cement. You may have to squash them down a little to make sure they do not bulge above the floor surface. But make sure they remain open enough to receive the wire. Two sets of wires are then fed into the conduit, as shown in Figure 41.

The set coming from the master bedroom should include two wires, each 15 inches in length. Run the wires through the conduit, allowing three inches to extend loosely onto the bedroom floor. Later, these two ends will be connected to the fixture wires we have already hidden under the bedroom wall covering. The set coming from the guestroom-study should be 12 inches in length. Run it through the shorter conduit, leaving three inches extending onto the floor of the guestroom-study. Both sets of wires come together at the corner of the stairwell and are allowed to dangle down through the well until they are connected to the rest of the wiring system below.

Our system does not call for ceiling lighting, but a more complex lighting system probably will. In such a case, the ceiling may also be routed as the floor was, and the conduit and wire positioned before the ceiling covering is glued on.

The purpose of the conduit is to make it easier to make

adjustments during the final wiring by moving the wires back and forth within the conduit. This flexibility is helpful but not crucial, and if you so choose, you may eliminate the conduit entirely and just glue the lengths of wire permanently into the routed grooves. Or you might lay them loosely in the grooves and attempt to lay the flooring over them, although this will be difficult.

Laying the Flooring

Different kinds of flooring can be selected for the different rooms, as in a real house. The easiest way of simulating hardwood floorboards is to scribe or rout parallel lines in the plywood surface and then stain it. But this also produces one of the least convincing effects because the very broad grain of the plywood shows through the stain and does not give a miniature appearance. A more effective result can be obtained by painting the plywood brown and then adding the parallel lines to represent boards. (See Figure 23 for some floorboard patterns.) You can also paint the floors and cover them with rugs and carpets of various sizes and colors, but this often gives too much of a patchwork or "busy" look, which interferes with the overall harmony of the decor.

For kitchens and hallways, tiny ¼-inch square ceramic tiles in geometric patterns are available from many craft shops. The tiles come attached to a net backing, so that they can be laid down in panels. The mortar, or "grout," can be washed across them to fill in the cracks. Regular-sized asphalt, vinyl, or rubber tiles can be cut down to miniature squares and laid down with the prescribed adhesive. Some vinyl tiles are made to resemble slate. However, you should try a sample first, since the slate effect does not always come down to dollhouse scale effectively.

There are various miniature stone, slate, and brick effects made especially to dollhouse scale and available at some retail outlets and through several of the suppliers listed in the Appendix. These are usually glued down and then brushed with glue and/or paint for a proper finish.

There are also paper simulations of miniature flooring of all sorts: parquet, Spanish tile, bathroom tile, etc. These should be lightly brushed with clear varnish after they are installed in order to give a used appearance.

Many early American colonists could not afford imported carpets or rugs and used, instead, painted canvas floor coverings. If your colonial is to be a strictly period house (which ours was not), you could use light canvas or sailcloth. First size it with two coats of white acrylic paint, and then paint miniature geometric or floral designs on it before finally gluing the finished covering to the floor.

After considerable study and experimentation, we decided to cover all our floors with fabric wall to wall, except for those in the attic and upstairs hallway, which we covered with basswood planking and real miniature hardwood flooring respectively.

As with wall coverings, carefully selected fabrics offer a surprisingly convincing effect of miniature texture and light absorbency. For our living room, we used a loosely woven wool fabric that was not tufted but nonetheless gave the effect of a wall-to-wall shag rug. The floors of the two second-story rooms were covered wall to wall in earth shades of very fine wool and polyester velvet. This gave the effect of finely tufted, nonshaggy carpeting.

All floor coverings follow the patterns of the original plywood floors, as shown in Figure 35. Note the two small rectangles in pattern A, First Floor, marked X and XX. These represent the positions of the fireplace (X) and the combination stairway box and wiring closet (XX). They should be clear of any fabric floor covering so that the fireplace and box can eventually be glued directly to the plywood.

By far the best wood flooring effect can be achieved by using real wood with a fine grain. To give the effect of plain plank flooring for the attic, we used basswood sheets 4 x 17 inches, scored with parallel planking lines made with the edge of a metal ruler. The sheets were glued to the plywood surface and then sanded and lightly rubbed with linseed oil to enrich the color. Do not varnish.

Miniature hardwood flooring is available from some doll-house shops and through several of the suppliers listed in the Appendix. It is offered in teak, maple, and mahogany, usually in packages containing enough tiny boards to cover 1 square foot. We chose teak for its mellow tone; mahogany is darker, and maple is redder. The manufacturers recommend laying the flooring down with contact cement, but since some contact cement dries bright yellow and is difficult to sand, we decided to use white glue, which dries clear and is easier to sand. After six months, our floor shows no sign of loosening.

We put hardwood flooring on the full length of the upstairs hall and ran the boards *across* the hallway. Start at the leading edge, that is, at the edge of the floor that will be the back of the dollhouse. Lay down only one or two boards at a time. Spread thin layers of glue on both the plywood and floorboard and allow it to dry partially for about three minutes. Then press the board into place. When you come to the grooves containing the wire or conduit, glue the boards over the grooves. Do your best to avoid having bulges of glue squeeze out of the cracks. When they do appear, quickly smooth them away with your finger. It will take an hour or more to lay the whole hallway, but the effect is worth the time. Allow the glue to dry thoroughly overnight, then sand it just enough to smooth the surface and remove any excess glue. Take care not to sand through the very thin boards. Clean away sanding dust with cotton swabs or a slightly damp cloth. The floor can be stained, but staining will darken it. We rubbed it with a coat of paste wax, allowed it to dry, rubbed in another coat, and then polished it. The result added a needed highlight and gave the whole floor an almost startling authenticity.

Making and Installing the Windows

You will need seven windows to fit 3-x-5-inch openings, and two windows to fit the 2-x-2-inch openings of the attic dormers. Windows can be purchased fully assembled; they can be put together from kits, or they can be made from scratch. For a basic do-it-yourself window, see Figure 21. X-acto offers an excellent window kit, available in many dollhouse outlets, for a nine-over-nine window in our dimensions. We made our own first- and second-story windows. For the attic dormers we purchased unfinished windows, to which we added plastic panes and basswood mullions. A variety of more elaborate windows, some of which open and close, are available in dollhouse shops and through some of the suppliers listed in the Appendix.

The same suppliers offer milled woodwork made expressly for windows, including window jambs, headers, sills, and routed casing. We used the plainer basswood lumber for our basic window, as shown in Figure 42.

66

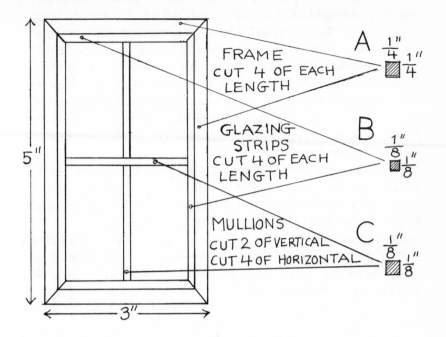

A FRAME
CUT 4 OF EACH
LENGTH
$\frac{1}{4}''$ $\frac{1}{4}''$

B GLAZING
STRIPS
CUT 4 OF EACH
LENGTH
$\frac{1}{8}''$ $\frac{1}{8}''$

C MULLIONS
CUT 2 OF VERTICAL
CUT 4 OF HORIZONTAL
$\frac{1}{8}''$ $\frac{1}{8}''$

5"

3"

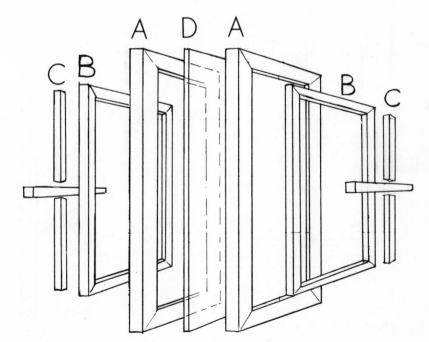

C B A D A B C

Figure 42

First cut all the parts. It is best to stain or paint them before assembly. Assemble two of the ¼-inch outside frames, A, using white glue. A flat toothpick is best for spreading glue on small areas. Next, cut the plastic or micro-glass pane, D. Measure it to the inside dimensions of the outer frame, or sandwich it between the two outer frames. (The latter method is shown in the diagram at the bottom of Figure 42.) Next, add the two inside frames of ⅛-inch glazing strips. Glue them into position on both sides of the pane to hold it in place. Finally, add two sets of mullions, one on each side of the pane.

Once the glue has set, place the window in the opening. If the assemblage is too large, sand down the outside edges. If you still have trouble getting the correct fit, try enlarging the opening with your utility knife and sandpaper. Next, glue the window into the opening. Make sure the inside is on the same plane as the inside wall of the house, and that the outside extends a fraction of an inch beyond the outside wall. The outside siding will eventually butt up against this extension.

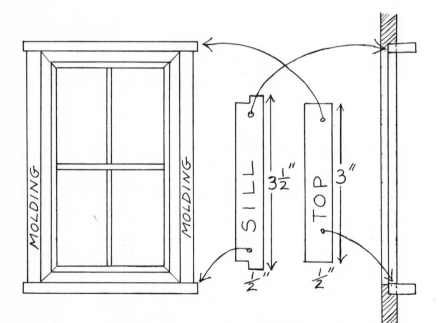

Figure 43

To finish each window on the inside, you can add strips of milled molding, ¼ x 1/16 inch, down each side, and on the sills at top and bottom, as shown in Figure 43.

To make the attic dormer windows from scratch, follow the same procedure, but use the dimensions indicated in Figure 56.

The construction of the two narrow windows flanking the front door is indicated in Figure 46. For further information, look in the Index under Windows.

Making and Hanging the Doors

You will need one front door and three inside doors. The door in the first-floor dividing wall, F, Figure 37, is an open arch. Doors can be purchased already assembled, they can be made from scratch (see Index under Doors), or they can be put together from kits. See the Appendix for suppliers who offer ready-made doors, including elaborately framed and columned front doorways.

We purchased four X-acto kits for doors measuring 3 x 6½ inches. One was used in the front door assembly and three for the inside doors on the second floor. The kits are available at most good hobby shops and dollhouse outlets. Similar wooden components for doors and frames are available by mail from some of the suppliers listed in the Appendix. You can use these components for making your doors, or you can even carve your own, patterning them after the parts shown in Figure 44.

The X-acto door has fifteen individual parts and is put together exactly like a full-sized door. Instructions are included in the kit. Take care and time with your first assembly effort in order to get the hang of it. Be particularly careful to use a minimum of white glue so that it will not bulge out and mar the door's appearance.

The X-acto door is illustrated in Figure 44. For a simpler door, see page 27.

HANGING THE DOORS

The X-acto kits come with tiny brass hinges and screws, but we found these difficult to install, particularly on the narrow edges

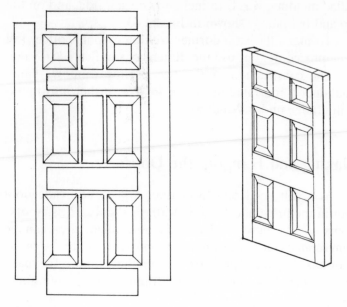

Figure 44

of ¼-inch dividing walls. Instead, we used an old and reliable method for hanging miniature doors, as shown in Figure 45. The method requires a frame completely enclosing the door. If you have routed the floors and ceilings to take the dividing walls, you will want to check the door frame dimensions and make sure the frame will clear the floor covering and allow the wall to be slid freely in and out. We routed the floor for our dividing walls, but decided to glue them in permanently. But we still had to cut down our doors ¼ inch at either end to fit them into the frame. Be prepared for a good deal of experimentation and adjustment before you are able to make your doors swing smoothly.

The method shown in Figure 45 is called post-hinging. Instead of turning on metal hinges, the door swivels on pegs at top and bottom. The pegs should be cut from a hard wood, such as 1/16-inch hardwood doweling in lengths of about 1 inch. We cut ours from a barbecue, or shish kebob, skewer made of bamboo, which is fibrous and tough. Drill two holes into the top and bottom of the hinge side of the door, as shown, A, taking care not to split the door. The holes should be no more than 1/16 inch wide and about ¾ of an inch deep. Glue the pegs into the holes, but be careful not to leave any glue bulging out, since it will

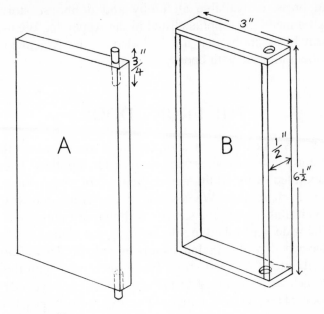

Figure 45

interfere with the swing of the door. The pegs should extend at bottom and top ¼ to ¾ inch.

Prepare the frames for the three upstairs doors using ¼-x-½-inch lumber in the lengths shown in the diagram. Make the frame for the front door from the wider ¼ x ¾ inch lumber. Sand the pieces lightly before gluing. Note the holes in the top and bottom pieces. These will be sockets for the pegs. Assemble the frame loosely, and insert the pegs into the sockets at top and bottom. Make sure the door will swing freely. If the fit is too tight, sand or cut the door down slightly. Position the two side pieces and glue the top to them. When the glue is dry, insert the door and its top peg in position, and then place the bottom piece of the frame so that the bottom peg is in its socket. Glue the bottom corners of the frame. Allow them to dry thoroughly, then glue the assembled pieces into the door opening. For the three interior doors and also the front door, the frame should be positioned so as to jut out ⅛ inch on both sides of the wall.

For the three interior doors, cover the joint between door frame and covered wall surface by adding flat framing of ¼-inch molding on both sides of the wall.

Miniature hardware for doors can be made from various

household items (see page 29). A variety of hardware, some made of real brass, is available at hobby and dollhouse stores and through some of the suppliers listed in the Appendix. We used the excellent brass knobs that are included in the X-acto kits and glued them in place with epoxy.

THE FRONT DOOR

Various kinds of front-door framings are available in dollhouse stores and through several mail-order suppliers. These can be elaborated with additional carpentry, or they can be put together from scratch. We assembled our front doorway from basswood lumber and pine scraps, as shown in Figure 46.

The wide jambs flanking the door, E, are made from ¼-x-¾-inch basswood, with beveled panels added for decoration. The overhead lintel, C, is made from ½-x-½-inch pine, with the 1/16-x-1/16-inch strip, B, added to the upper leading edge. (Or use a basswood plank, 1/16 x 1 inch.) The two outside posts, D, are made from ¼-x-¼-inch basswood. The lower window panels, I,

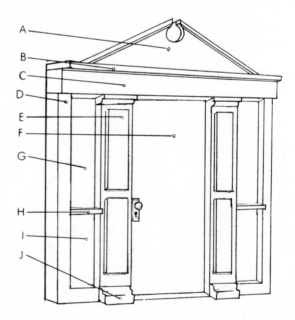

Figure 46

are filled in with pine scraps. Small sills of 1/16-x-½-inch basswood are added to the bottoms of the two narrow windows, H. Two panes of colored plastic (we used amber) are glazed in, G, using 1/16-x-1/16-inch basswood glazing strips. They are also secured with similar glazing strips on the inside. The overhead peaked cornice, A, is cut from a ¼-inch-thick scrap of basswood in the pattern shown, and elaborated with small strips of scrap wood. Lay it aside until the siding is glued onto the outside of the shell, at which time it can be positioned and glued into place over the siding. If you decide not to use siding but to paint the exterior instead, add the cornice to the doorway now.

The decorative bottom sills, J, are cut from a length of regular molding purchased at a lumber yard.

Hardware for front doors includes a variety of knobs and handles, door knockers, bells, and name plates. They are available at dollhouse outlets and through suppliers listed in the Appendix.

The inside of the front door and the insides of the windows are finished with flat framing of ¼-x-1/16-inch molding.

Before you assemble the shell and complete and install the wiring system, you must begin construction of the main stairway, since its platform also serves as a closet to hide the wiring transformer and fuse system. The upstairs stairway should be built as well.

Building the Main Stairway

As you can see in Figure 48, the main stairway consists of two flights interrupted by a platform, which also serves as a closet. The closet door faces the open rear of the dollhouse. This platform box will contain the wiring transformer and fuse system. (Some systems locate the transformer in the attic.)

Build the platform box with ¼-inch plywood in the dimensions shown, A, Figure 47. The side that will go next to the dividing wall can be left open. Note the hole in the bottom, which is meant to coincide with the basement opening in the first-floor plywood panel, Figure 35, A. Put the box together with white glue. A door may be added and hung in place (A, Figure 48), using the method described on page 27.

The two flights of the stairway are built separately. The first flight is constructed as shown in H, Figure 47, and in H, Figure 48.

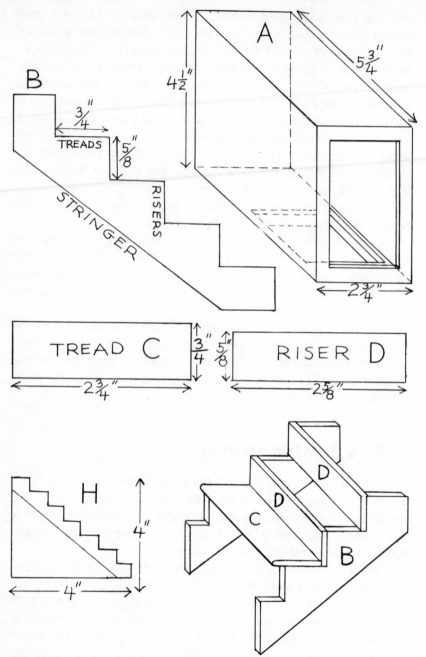

Figure 47

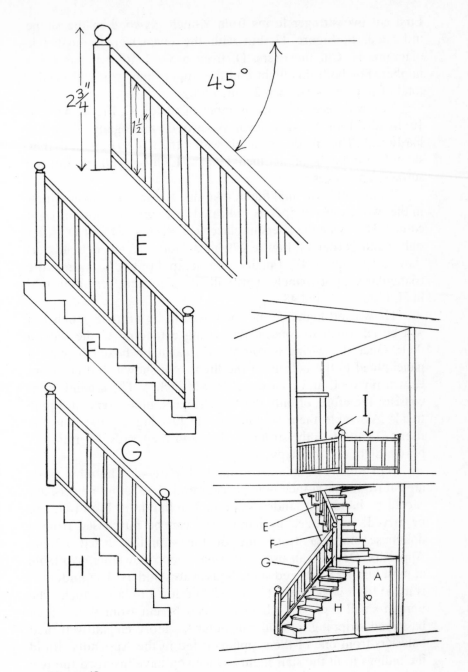

$2\frac{3}{4}''$

$1\frac{1}{2}''$

45°

E

F

G

H

I

E
F
G
A
H

Figure 48

First cut two stringer forms from ¼-inch plywood in the shape indicated, B, Figure 47, but with the seven steps indicated in diagrams H. Cut the risers, D, from 5/8-x-1/16-inch basswood lumber. For both this flight and the upper flight you will need a total of sixteen risers, each 2⅝ inch long.

You will need the same number of treads, C, Figure 47. Cut 16 treads from ¾-x-1/16-inch basswood, mahogany, or other hardwood. The treads are a bit wider than the risers and they should also be ⅛ of an inch longer. Lightly sand all outside surfaces and edges.

To assemble the first flight, first glue the seven bottom panels to the two stringer shapes as indicated in Figure 47, bottom right corner. Then glue the risers in place, as indicated, D and D, lower right-hand corner of Figure 47. Next, add the seven treads, as shown, C, Figure 47. Finally, use scrap lumber to frame the triangular support panels. This will complete the form indicated in H, Figures 47 and 48.

The second flight will not be boxed in by support panels but will be left open to conceal the wiring extending to the second floor. Once the wiring is completed, it can be boxed in with a panel glued to the bottom of the flight (not shown) but cut from ¼-inch plywood and measuring 2¾ x 8 inches. The second flight consists, therefore, of only the two stringers, nine risers, and nine treads. Assemble them as you did the first flight. First glue the risers, D and D, to the stringers, then add the treads, C, until you have a flight of nine steps.

Stair rails are made according to Figure 48. The main posts are cut from ¼-x-¼-inch pine or basswood. The round newels, are carved by hand and sanded smooth. The handrail, E and G, can be carved and sanded by hand, or it can be purchased from a dollhouse store or from one of the suppliers listed in the Appendix. Or you can use ¼-inch hardwood doweling, available at most lumber yards and some housewares outlets. The underrail is made from ¼-x-¼-inch basswood, cut down to ¼ x ⅛ inch. The upright smaller posts, or balusters, can be cut from ⅛-x-⅛-inch basswood stripping, or you can purchase more elegantly turned balusters from one of the suppliers listed in the Appendix. Build the railings to fit the stair flights. Once you have installed the two flights and their rails, you can measure and build the two sections of railing for the stairwell on the second floor, I, Figure 48.

To finish the stairway, first stain the treads, handrails, and main posts of all sections with mahogany or maple stain (or better yet, use the materials from the X-acto furniture-finishing kit). Then use acrylic or latex white to paint all other parts: risers, stringers, bottom rails, balusters, and panels.

Building the Attic Stairway

The simplest way to install a stairway from the second floor to the attic is to run a straight flight of stairs directly up from the second-floor hallway. You can build it as suggested in Figure 47 but with a total of thirteen steps. If this is your choice, you should shorten the stairwell opening in the attic-floor panel, C, Figure 35, by at least 3 inches, measuring from the end near the rear of the

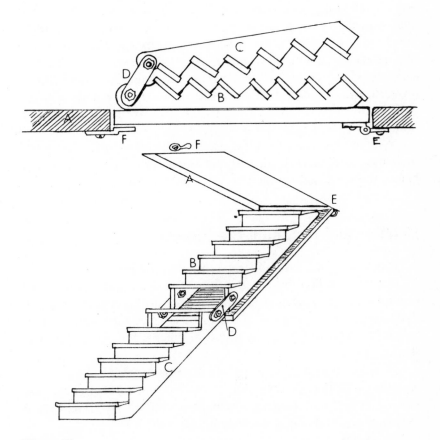

Figure 49

dollhouse. This stairway should also be narrower than the main stairway, with risers only 2 inches long; the treads should measure 2⅛ inches in length. The treads need not be made from hardwood. Handrails can be simpler to construct. You need not stain any of the parts but may paint the whole stairway white.

Since such a stairway tends to crowd the hallway, we chose to put together the folding and "disappearing" stairway shown in Figure 49. It can be pulled down from the ceiling so that its bottom legs rest on the hallway floor beside the main stairwell. When it is not in use, it can be folded and recessed in the attic stairwell opening, held in place by the small latch, F. The stairs themselves are made as indicated in Figure 47, but with 2-inch-long risers and treads. There are two sections, C and B, the first with six steps, the second with seven steps. These are first hinged with plates made of thin aluminum, D, and held in place by small bolts. The folding stairs are then glued to a plywood panel 8 x 2¾ inches, in the manner shown in the drawing. This panel is then hinged in position, E, so that it becomes a trap door that closes the attic stairwell; the folded ladder rests on top of it. When the stairway is lowered, the catch, F, is moved aside. The panel is then lowered, and the second section of the stairway is folded outward and down to the hallway floor to take the form shown in the bottom drawing, Figure 49.

You may choose to build and install this stairway after the shell has been assembled. But the main stairway must be built before the shell is assembled and the electric wiring is completed.

Building and Installing the Fireplace

Some fireplace assemblies extend onto the wall and therefore should be installed before the house shell is assembled. For example, X-acto makes a kit for an elegant Georgian fireplace that extends to the ceiling. On the other hand, our fireplace is a simple one and can be easily glued in place after assembling the shell.

Fireplaces can be bought ready-made; they can be put together from kits, or they can be made from scratch. They are usually made with wooden shells, but can be covered with a variety of textural effects, including brick and stone. Consult both the Index and the Appendix.

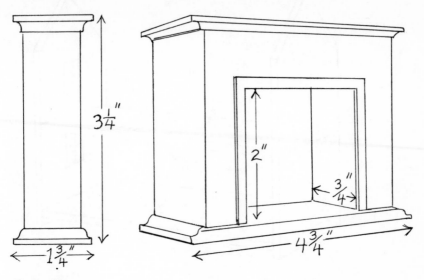

Figure 50

Our fireplace follows the dimensions shown in Figure 50. Cut the side, front, and top panels from ¼-inch ply and glue together. Cut the smaller panels of the firebox from ¼-inch ply and glue them into position. Add details made of basswood scraps or milled molding. The topmost mantel panel can be made with maple or mahogany. To finish, stain the mantel, paint the rest of the woodwork white, and paint the inside surfaces of the firebox matte black.

Andirons and other fireplace hardware are available at dollhouse outlets and through suppliers listed in the Appendix. You can carve your own andirons and tongs from wood and paint them black or gold, or you can make them with bits of metal, glued together with epoxy.

You are now ready to assemble the shell of the house.

Assembling the Shell

You will need another pair of hands to help with the first steps of assembly. First, prepare to assemble the ½-inch ply frame, A in Figure 51. Put glue along the edges of the three floor panels and along the floor lines on the two peaked end panels. Contact

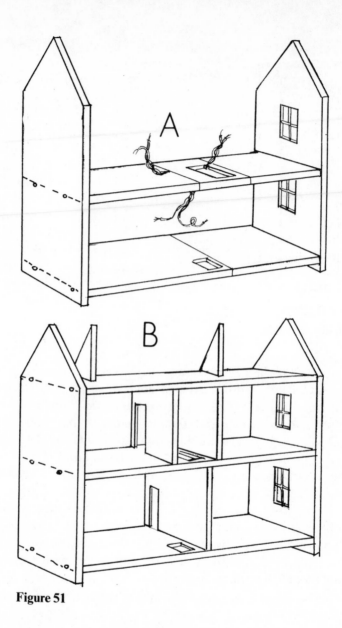

Figure 51

glue is excellent, but you must take great care that it does not dribble down the wall covering of an inside wall. Try not to spread it so thickly that it will squeeze out into bulges. White glue does not make as immediate a bond as contact cement, but it is easier to handle. While allowing the glue to dry partially, reinsert the nails that you removed from your first temporary assembly. (If you are using wood screws, set them into the end-wall floor lines, as indicated by the little circles in the diagram.) Start with the bottom floor, and have your partner hold the floor and wall in place, while you drive in the nails or set the screws. Then do the other end of the floor. Next, insert the second floor, taking care to line it up exactly on the floor lines on the end wall. Align and nail or screw. Repeat this process for the third floor.

Try the frame on an even surface, taking care not to exert too much pressure end to end. It will sway from end to end if pushed, but if it does not rest evenly on the floor, see if a small amount of pressure at the proper corner will align the frame. If it continues to rest unevenly on the floor, you may have to pull out one or more floors and make adjustments. Sometimes a small wedge under one bottom corner of an end wall will bring the frame into line. Take all the time you need to make sure this basic frame is right.

When you think ,the frame is ready, prepare the large windowed façade panel, L, Figure 36. Apply glue to the three floor lines and to the edges of each end. Apply glue to the leading edges of the front of the basic frame. To do this, you should carefully turn the frame over on its back. While the glue is partially drying, set brads or very small screws at the four corners of the façade, positioning them so that they will eventually penetrate the frame edge. Place the façade in position on the front, upper edge of the frame, and make sure that the frame is square and that the façade matches it almost perfectly. Take particular care to see that the lower corners are aligned; the upper corners will be slightly hidden by the overhang of the roof when the roof is installed.

Nail the façade (or use small screws) with brads placed every 2 or 3 inches along all lines where the façade and frame make contact. Give the glue plenty of time to dry before proceeding.

The next step in the assembly process, the placing of the dividing walls, is illustrated in diagram B, Figure 51, and in Figure 28 at the beginning of this chapter. If you plan to make the first and second floor dividing walls removable, you may merely slide them into their routed grooves. Or you can glue them in, taking care to allow only a minimum of glue to bulge out onto the floor and wall coverings.

Completing the Wiring Systems and Components

Even a minimum of lighting brings a dollhouse alive. It breaks up the steady outside source of light into smaller patterns of light and shade; the interior resembles a world unto itself. You can wire the house for a complete complement of overhead lights, standing lamps, and table lamps. You can install a simple system of indirect display lighting, as we did. Or you can choose something in between. Before you make your choice, read through our description of basic wiring.

Complete dollhouse wiring systems are for sale in dollhouse stores and are available through suppliers listed in the Appendix. There are systems for basic wiring and for a variety of elaborations. Also available are strings of Christmas tree lights with small, clear or frosted bulbs and a built-in transformer. The best way to cut costs is to install your own system.

However simple or elaborate the lighting plan, it will require similar basic components: a transformer, a fuse holder and fuse, lengths of small-gauge wire, and bulbs or lamps.

The transformer, A, Figure 52, is a device that transforms or

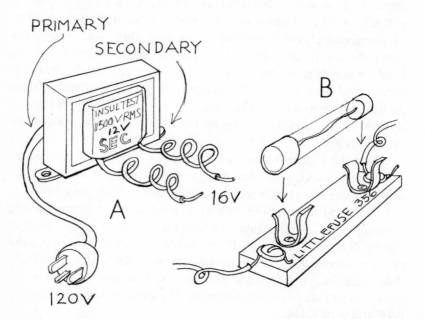

Figure 52

reduces electrical power. Because dollhouse wiring and fixtures are miniaturized, they are more delicate than regular house wiring. They would quickly burn out if they received the full force of the power available from your house's system. The transformer takes in the electricity from your wall outlet, reduces it in power, and sends it on into your dollhouse system as a more manageable and safer electric force. For our purposes here, electrical power is measured in voltage. The juice (a more expressive term than electricity) enters the transformer at 115 or 120 volts and comes out at about 12 volts. The lower voltage is less likely to burn out the dollhouse wiring system and start a fire, and it poses little physical danger to you. In fact, the shock from 12 volts is virtually harmless to human beings, young or old. Keep in mind, however, that the shock from the primary side of the transformer is 120 volts and dangerous.

Most dollhouse lights are able to take 16 volts. But because miniature bulbs are so delicate, the best way to keep them working to their full life expectancy is to use them at a lower voltage. Therefore, we recommend using a 12-volt transformer. Such small transformers are used to activate door chimes and are available in most hardware stores. Both 14- and 16-volt transformers will work, but they will burn out your bulbs sooner than will a 12-volt transformer. A 10-volt transformer can be used, since it actually delivers between 12 and 14 volts.

Every transformer has two sets of wiring poles, called secondary and primary. The primary connection is for the wires that will plug into the 120-volt wall socket. The secondary connection is for the wires that will carry 12 volts into your dollhouse system. These poles should be clearly marked on the transformer casing as PRIM and SEC. Usually the PRIM connection already has two wires that protrude from the casing. The SEC connection may be another set of wires, or it may be only a set of poles with screw-down connections.

For our system we used only one 12-volt transformer. A more elaborate system, using twenty or more lights, requires two transformers.

To be absolutely safe, it is wise to also install a fuse holder and fuse, diagram B, Figure 52. This is an interruption in the system, bridged by a glass capsule, or fuse, containing a metal filament that will burn away when the amount of electrical charge in the system exceeds 12 volts. Before the wires or fixtures can become hot enough to pose a fire danger, the fuse will blow and the flow of current will be cut off. A fuse is a kind of safety valve.

Such small fuse systems are used for safeguarding automotive wiring, and they can be found in some automobile parts stores. They can also be purchased at dollhouse and hobby shops or ordered from suppliers listed in our Appendix. Get a fuse that is rated at 1500 milliamperes. We needed only one fuse holder with a fuse. A system that uses two transformers requires two fuse systems.

Most dollhouses are wired in what is called "series." The juice travels on a circuit—that is, in a circle. Light bulbs are inserted into this circle of power, but they do not allow the power to pass through as easily as the wires do. The current passes through them along a metal filament, which offers some resistance to its passage. As a result, the filament heats up and glows, and we have light.

Wire is available in solid or stranded forms. The first kind has a single, relatively thick wire running inside the insulation sheathing; the second has several thinner strands of wire. Stranded wire is best because it is more flexible and less likely to kink and break. Buy wire rated to take 16 volts—available at some dollhouse stores and through the suppliers listed in the Appendix. Get the narrowest wire available; it is easier to conceal, and when it does show, it is more nearly in scale. For our limited display system you will need about 16 feet of wire. For convenience during the wiring operation (provided you plan to hide most of your wiring), try to get half of your wire with white insulation, half with black or red insulation.

Light bulbs are available in three forms: screw-in bulbs, grain-of-wheat bulbs, and tubular fluorettes. They can be acquired at some hardware and automotive stores, at dollhouse outlets, or from the suppliers listed in the Appendix. Screw-in bulbs have the advantage of being easily removed for replacement, but the socket system makes them bulkier than grain-of-wheat bulbs. The grain-of-wheat bulb is tiny and has two wires coming directly from it. Although it is smaller, it is more difficult to replace, since the wires must be cut and the new bulb soldered in place again. Both types are available, with various voltage ratings, but 12- to 16-volt ratings are best for dollhouse use.

For our display system we used fluorettes (see Figure 54–7). They are tubular in form and are easily clipped in or out of a

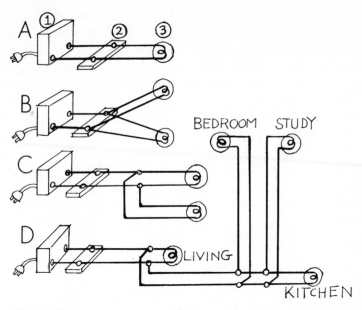

Figure 53

special socket, which has solder terminals for connection to the wiring system. These are 16-volt bulbs that consume 80 milliamperes and should be used with a 12-volt transformer.

In the basic wiring circuit, the components are connected as shown in diagram A, Figure 53. No. 1 is the transformer, No. 2 is the fuse holder and fuse, and No. 3 is the bulb. One wire goes from one of the SEC poles of the transformer to one pole of the fuse holder and from there to one solder terminal of the bulb holder. The other wire goes from the other SEC pole of the transformer to the other pole of the fuse holder and from there to the other solder terminal of the bulb holder. As you can see, the circuit is closed within the bulb by the curlicue of filament. This basic circuit is sufficient to light one bulb.

Extra bulbs can be wired into the basic circuit, as indicated in B, or as shown in C. Our system was a further elaboration of C, sufficient to light up four lumette bulbs, diagramed in D.

For more complex systems, two kinds of wires are needed, plus terminal strips, and sometimes a second transformer and fuse system. Ceiling, wall, and floor lamps for elaborate systems are available in dollhouse outlets and through the suppliers listed in the Appendix. Some are completely wired and assembled; some require assembling. If you decide to install a more elaborate system than ours, we recommend that you send a letter and a self-addressed, stamped envelope to Ed Leonard of Illinois Hobbycraft (listed in the Appendix). Request his price lists and excellent technical bulletins, which give complete details on the construction of a complex lighting system. Or you can purchase an already completed system at one of the better dollhouse stores.

From this point on, we will be discussing only our limited system. It is not designed to give a detailed lighting effect, but rather to indirectly illuminate the interior furnishings and give the effect of a home with the lights dimmed (probably an hour or so before bedtime).

FLUORETTE LIGHT FIXTURE

Before you install the wiring, it is best to assemble your four light fixtures. For three of the fluorette bulb holders we devised a simple light shade designed to fit over the bulb holder, which was then fixed to the wall, as indicated in Figure 54. The bulb holder, A, is a simple fiber plate with metal clamps at either end to hold the bulb, and a soldering point at either end of the plate. Use epoxy or contact cement to fix the holder to a piece of ⅛-x-¾-inch pine or basswood, as shown in diagram A, Figure 54. Then cut out the pieces of the shade, 1, 2, 3, and 4, from 1/16-inch-thick basswood or balsa wood. Assemble the shade as shown, then glue. Glue a small sheet of aluminum foil inside each shade to prevent overheating of the wood and to increase the fixture's reflective qualities. The shade can be covered with material identical to that used for the wall on which it is to be hung, or it can be painted white or any color of your choice. The bulb holder and its wooden backing are then mounted on the wall so that the narrow strip, 6, holds the top part of the plate ¼ inch away from the wall surface. This enables the shade to be slipped down over the holder, as indicated, B. The fourth bulb holder will be mounted on the inside top edge of the stairway box, under the stairs, and will be covered later with a plastic panel.

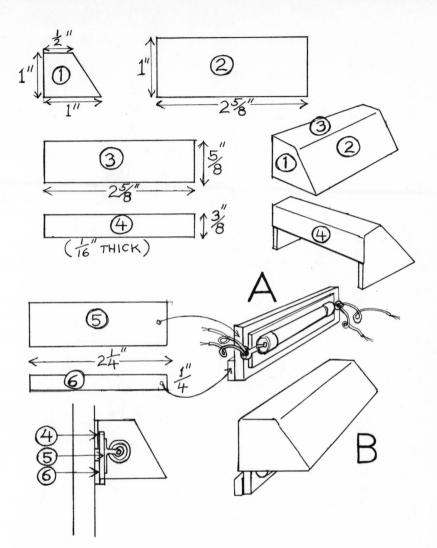

Figure 54

ASSEMBLING THE WIRING SYSTEM

The system is diagramed with side and rear views in Figure 55. Compare these diagrams with Figures 28, 41, and 48 to get a picture of how the wiring system relates to the overall structure of the house and stairway. The stairway components are ready but

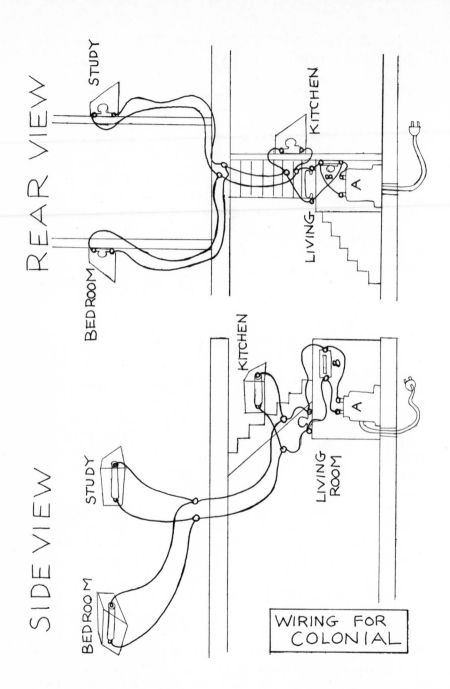

Figure 55

88

unassembled. The stairway platform box, A, Figure 48, will now become an integral part of the wiring system.

First mount the transformer, A, inside the stair box with the SEC power poles facing toward the box door—that is, toward the back of the house. Use screws, bolts, or epoxy glue to hold the transformer in place. If the device has no feet, use only epoxy. To the PRIM wires, splice a 4-foot or longer length of household electrical cord with a regular socket plug at the end. Be sure to wrap the splice well with electrician's tape. This PRIM line (120 volts) will be dropped down through the floor of the box and house and placed along the bottom of the first-floor panel through the "foundation" of the house. It will then be drawn through a hole in the end panel with the windows, and thence to your wall outlet.

Next, position the fuse holder, B, just inside the box door and attach it to the inside box wall with a screw or epoxy. Run two short wires from the two soldering points of the fuse holder to the two SEC poles of the transformer. Solder all four points, using wire solder with a flux core. If you have never used a soldering iron before, practice a few times with spare pieces of wire twisted together. The secret lies in not trying to push or smear the solder. Using the tip of the iron, first heat up the connection or the twist of wires to be sealed. Then move the soldering wire in close to the iron, holding both slightly above the connection. Allow the heat from the iron to form a bead of molten solder. Gently drop the bead onto the connection, letting the solder enclose the connection at the instant that it begins to cool and harden.

Next, wire in the living room light. First position the bulb holder on the top rear of the box (under the second flight of stairs). Attach each of the two wires to a SEC pole, then pass it through a hole in the rear top of the box. Finally, wire it to a pole of the bulb holder.

Next, drill a small hole in the dividing wall between the living room and kitchen, at the height where you expect to install the kitchen fixture. Put the wall in place. Wire the kitchen fixture to the living room fixture. Attach the wires to the kitchen fixture first, then solder. Then pull the wires tight enough to hold the fixture in its final position. Attach the other ends of the wires to the living room fixture's soldering points. Make the wires as tight as possible, but keep in mind that any slack can be concealed later under the second stair flight. Do not solder the living room points yet.

Now wire in the two upstairs fixtures. In each case, start first with the wall fixture. Solder the points and glue the fixture into place on the wall. Next, attach the downstairs ends of the wires to the living room fixture, as you did with the kitchen wires. Pull the wires as tight as you can without pulling something else loose, and move the loose stair box about as needed.

Before the final soldering, give the system its first test. Put fluorette bulbs into each of the four fixtures. Insert the 16-volt fuse in its holder. Plug the PRIM transformer cord into your 120-volt wall outlet.

If the lights do not go on, you may have a loose connection, or a bare wire may be touching another wire somewhere, causing a short circuit. Before checking, disconnect the PRIM contact and pull the plug from the wall socket. Look at the fuse; any serious short should have blown it out. If the fine wire inside the fuse's glass tube is still intact, examine all your connections for looseness. Somewhere a wire is not making contact, or one of your fluorette bulbs is faulty or burned out.

Once you are sure the system is functioning correctly, disconnect the PRIM power cord from the wall socket. Solder all points, making sure that all the connections to the living room fixture are closed and protected by the solder.

Finally, put the other elements of the stairway loosely in place to make sure the slope of the upper flight conceals the living room fixture and its many connections. Any slack wires can be taken up by kinking or doubling back the wires and binding with electrician's tape.

Plug the PRIM cord in and test the system a second time.

You are now ready to install the rest of the stairway. Unplug the PRIM cord to cut off the power while you work.

Installing the Stairways

First glue the stairbox into position, taking care to let the PRIM cord of the transformer dangle down through the "basement" hole in the first-floor panel. Glue the box at the bottom and on the edges next to the dividing wall, as shown in Figure 48. Next, glue the first flight, H, into position, ¾ inch in from the rear edge of the first-floor panel. Next, glue the second flight into position. Its lower end should rest 3 inches in from the leading (rear of house) edge of the box, and its top edge should be flush with the second-story hallway floor. For a snug fit, you may have to add a strip of wood down the inside of the upper flight. Then mount the balustrades, starting with the first flight. Proceed to the second, and then finish with the railing that goes around the stairwell on the second floor.

Before the glue has entirely dried, plug the PRIM cord of your wiring system back into the wall outlet and check the lighting one final time. If there is something wrong, you can make a drastic retreat by quickly taking out the stair flights and repairing the wiring.

Finally, cut a panel of ¼-inch plywood the same size as the bottom of the second flight. Put it in place and push the wiring up

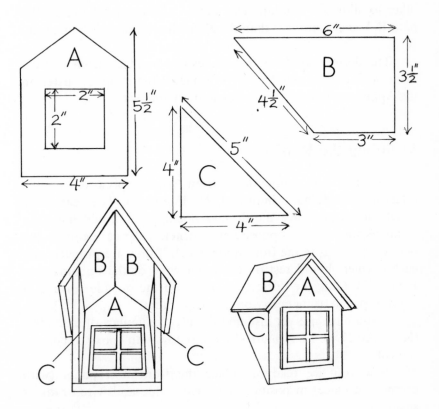

Figure 56

under the stairs in order to conceal it. Leave an opening large enough for the living room fixture to spill its light out into the room from its position on the end of the box under the stairs. Complete the installation by adding a panel of clear or frosted plastic or micro-glass.

Next, install the attic stairway, either as a permanent structure or as a folding stairway.

Before you can install the roof, the attic dormers must be built and glued in place on the front roof panel, M, Figure 34.

Building and Installing the Dormers

Cut the dormer pieces from ¼-inch plywood in the dimensions shown in Figure 56. Cut two sets, or a total of ten pieces. Notice that one side of each dormer roof is a bit wider than the other to allow for overlap. This means you must cut two of the part, B, ¼ inch narrower than the 3½ inches indicated in diagram, B.

The dormer windows themselves can be made from scratch, made with kits, or purchased from one of the suppliers listed in the Appendix. Consult the Index under windows.

Installing the Roof

Cut the front roof slope from ¼-inch plywood in the dimensions and shape indicated, M, Figure 34. The rear slope panel should not have the dormer opening; it should have the chimney notch in the opposite end corner. Take care cutting the dormer openings in the front slope panel. If they are properly cut, each dormer should rest on the outer edge of the opening (see Figure 57). Glue the dormers in place on the outside surface of the roof panel, using epoxy or contact cement.

If you have not yet installed the two triangular attic dividers (K, Figure 37, and K, Figure 40), do so now with epoxy or contact cement.

Now you are ready to place the front roof panel (with dormers in place) in position. Use white glue and wire brads or small screws.

The rear roof panel (with no dormers) should be hinged to the front panel, as indicated in Figure 58. Use epoxy as well as the

Figure 57

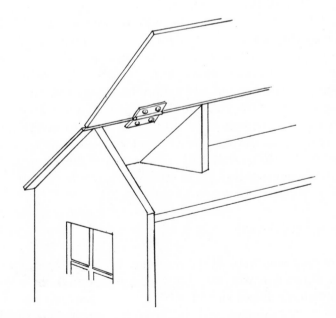

Figure 58

screws and file the screw points down to the panel surface. The rear roof panel can now be lifted up to reveal the interior of the attic, or it can be lowered to form a normal roof at the rear of the house.

Before shingling the roof and putting siding on the outside of the house, you should construct and install the chimney.

Building and Installing the Chimney

You can, if you wish, make a narrower and simpler chimney than the one presented here. However, since this house is decorated simply (we have not included shutters), a massive chimney will give it added dignity at little extra cost. Cut the shapes shown in Figure 59 from ¼-inch plywood. Note that some of the parts are to be cut in multiples. Sand all parts lightly and assemble as shown. Glue with white glue and secure with fine 1-inch wire brads. Drive them carefully into the delicate ply. Allow the glue to dry thoroughly, and then sand all the edges to remove the glue and round off the corners. If the joints remain uneven after sanding, you may want to add a thin coat of plaster of paris or spackle and carefully fill in all cracks and pits. Allow the plaster to dry and then lightly sand again.

Glue the chimney to the end wall without windows. White glue will do, but epoxy is better for this job. Once the glue has dried, use plaster of paris or plastic wood to fill in any gaps between shell and wall. Plastic wood will prove to be particularly helpful in concealing the join at the top where the chimney hooks over the peak of the roof. If you do not plan to add siding to the outside of the house, you will want to do a more thorough job of plastering the join between chimney and house. If you do plan to add siding, the siding will help you to cover the smaller gaps between chimney and wall.

Finishing the Roof

You may want to paint the roof and then draw black shingle outlines on it. Or you can cut miniature courses of asphalt shingling from sandpaper and glue them in place, as shown in Figure 26. Another quick and cheap roofing can be made by first

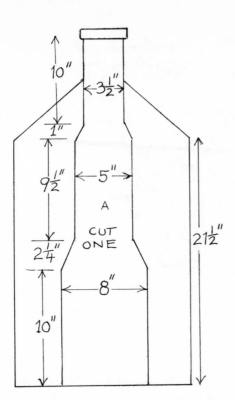

10"

3½"

1"

9½"

5"

A

CUT
ONE

2¼"

8"

10"

21½"

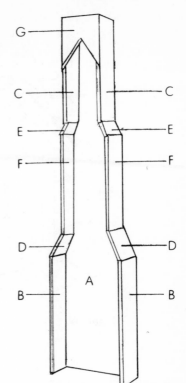

G

C ——— C

E ——— E

F ——— F

D ——— D

B ——— B

A

B
AND
C

CUT
FOUR

10"

2"

D
CUT
TWO

2¾"

2"

E
CUT
TWO

2" 1⅛"

F
CUT
TWO

9½"

2"

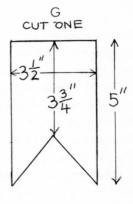

G
CUT ONE

3½"

3¾"

5"

Figure 59

95

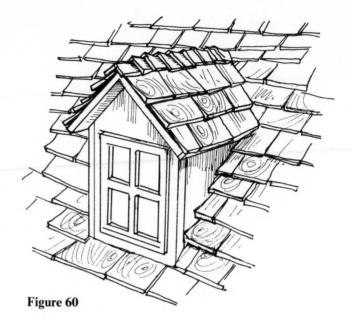

Figure 60

brushing on a medium-thick coat of white glue. Allow the glue to become tacky, then sprinkle it with clean white sand or black grit for a tar-and-sand effect. If you have vinyl imitation slate floor tiles available, they can be cut into small squares and glued on as miniature slate shingles.

We used miniature cedar shingles. They are sold at most dollhouse stores and can be ordered from the suppliers listed in the Appendix. They usually come in bags containing enough shingles to cover 1 square foot. The roof of this Colonial measures about 6½ square feet, including the dormer roofs. Check the price carefully before deciding to use them; they are not cheap. Glue the shingles to the roof with contact cement, positioning them as indicated in Figure 60. Start by laying the bottom course first, and place the shingles along the full length of the roof before you start a new course. Lap the shingles of the second course about ½ inch over the tops of those of the first course. Pay special attention to the arrangement of shingles along the ridge of each dormer, as shown in Figure 60. Notice that the top course of shingles running along the peak have been split in half before being put in place.

The shingles from the two slopes of the larger roof panels

should not quite meet at the peak. Leave a ¼- to ⅛-inch gap along the peak to allow the rear roof panel to swing freely upward.

Applying Siding to the Outside Walls

There are a number of ways to finish the outside walls of the Colonial. The cheapest and quickest way is simply to paint the outside walls white or the color of your choice. Or you can paint and then draw black or brown lines to indicate clapboard siding or shingling. You can cut shingles from sandpaper (see Figure 26) and glue them on the walls as you would on a rooftop. Begin from the bottom and work upward. You can paint the walls a stone color and then scribe the paint to simulate stones or bricks. You can apply a thin coat of plaster and, while it is still damp, scribe lines to represent stones or brick and paint them when the plaster has dried. You can use one of the commercial stick-on stone or brick effects sold in dollhouse stores and available through suppliers listed in the Appendix. See Index under Stone and Brick effects.

You can make individual clapboards from basswood strips

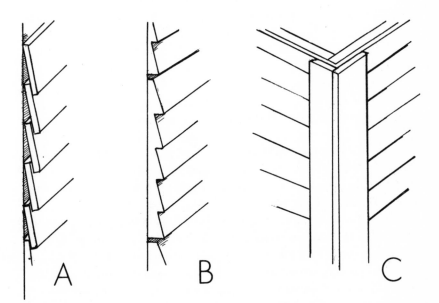

A   B   C

Figure 61

approximately 1/16 inch thick by ½ (or ⅝) inch wide. These should be glued on starting at the bottom of each wall and lapping ⅛ inch of the top board over the top edge of the bottom board, as shown, A, Figure 61.

We purchased ready-made clapboard siding, B. It comes in sheets of various sizes, usually with several lengths of board to a sheet. Try your local dollhouse outlet or one of the mail suppliers listed in the Appendix.

Work slowly and carefully, making your siding fit as closely as possible to the window frames. Fill in cracks and mistakes with plaster of paris or plastic wood. You may need to add some extra wood trim around some windows to give the carpentry a finished look. At each corner, add 1/16-x-⅝-inch wood strips, as shown, C, in Figure 61.

Painting

Latex indoor paint will do, but a good acrylic, such as TACC, is best. Be very careful to leave as few brush marks as possible. In miniature, all such flaws stand out. Apply one coat of paint, allow it to dry thoroughly, then apply a second coat. A third coat ensures a surface that will last for years. Be sure to use a matte, or nonglossy, paint.

Paint whatever trim you wish. We painted only the front door and window frames in charcoal gray.

Finishing the Foundation

The foundation line runs around the base of our Colonial at about 2 inches above the bottom edge of the house. The line can be painted gray or it can be finished with various stone-and-brick methods. Consult the Index.

We used Doreen Sinnett's brick sheeting, listed in the Appendix. It comes in small sheets that can be cut with scissors or a craft knife, which makes it easy to fit one sheet to another and to carry the correct brick pattern around the corners (see Figure 62). You can also cut out individual bricks and create a herringbone or other pattern. The sheeting is first glued to the surface and

Figure 62

allowed to dry. It is then coated with thinned white glue for chip resistance. The sheeting is available in an attractive brick-red color, but it can be painted as well.

Making and Installing the Shutters

For simplicity's sake, and to hold down costs, we have not hung shutters on our Colonial. However, most Colonials do have shutters. Shutters of all kinds, Figure 63, including elaborately louvered models, are available in dollhouse outlets and through the suppliers listed in the Appendix. For homemade shutters, consult the Index.

Building the Front Porch and Steps

We constructed our front steps from ¼-inch plywood, following the pattern suggested in Figure 64. Because such a stairway could easily break loose from the body of the dollhouse, we have built it as a separate unit. It can, of course, be attached, preferably with epoxy glue. We used ¼-inch doweling for the handrail and small bamboo barbecue skewers for the upright spindles. Once the railings are glued together, paint them with matte black for a wrought-iron effect.

The flower boxes were constructed from basswood scraps.

99

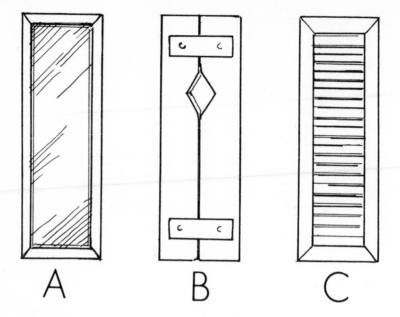

A   B   C

Figure 63

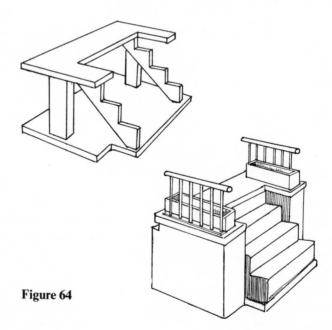

Figure 64

The boxes were filled with damp potter's clay (you can use modeling clay or play-dough). Miniature dried flowers from a local florist's were cut, and their stems were pushed into the clay.

Final Details

At the rear of the house, the leading edges of floors and walls are still exposed. Cut strips of basswood or pine in the proper dimensions and glue them with contact cement to cover their edges. Sand the strips to round them slightly. They can be stained, painted, or varnished. We left ours natural, then rubbed them with paste wax to keep the dirt out.

Paste wax will also deepen the color and protect the surface of the hardwood flooring in the upstairs hallway.

Strips of miniature basswood molding can be glued around the bottoms of the inside walls. Such molding is available in different shapes from dollhouse outlets and through the suppliers listed in the Appendix.

The stairbox on the first floor can be equipped with a small door, as shown in Figure 48, A, to allow access to the fuse holder and transformer. If you wish the door to double as a basement entrance, paint the interior of the stairbox matte black and install a short flight of steps, which will seem to disappear downward into darkness.

Run the power line from the transformer under the bottom floor and hold it in place with brackets. We made our brackets from folded sheet rubber to keep the cord from being rubbed; if you use metal brackets, tape them with electrician's tape to help protect the cord's insulation. Trail the power cord through a hole in the foundation base of the fireplace end of the house. To avoid having to continually plug and unplug the power cord, you can wire in an on-off switch, either into the power line or into an on-off switch attached to the foundation wall at the base of the chimney.

To protect the interior and furnishing of your Colonial, you can cut a panel of acrylite, Perma Glaze II, or other clear plastic or glass and mount it on brackets to make a removable see-through shield covering the entire open area at the rear of the house.

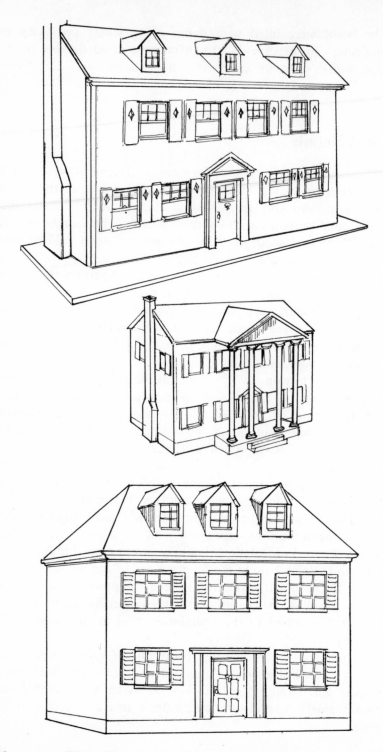

102   **Figure 65**

Finally, mount the house on a panel with attached revolving castors, or even on a large lazy susan, in order to allow the house to be turned around easily.

ALTERNATIVE DESIGNS

The basic shell of this Colonial can be kept simple or it can be more elaborate. Extra windows can be added. See the top of Figure 65 for the Williamsburg Colonial pattern for a pair of windows at either side of the front door, five windows upstairs, and three attic dormers. The addition of a columned portico can turn the basic Colonial into a stately Southern mansion. An authentic Dutch Colonial effect can be achieved by transforming the pitched roof to a hip roof, as suggested at the bottom of Figure 64. The basic shell could become a Victorian house with the addition of a tower.

CONGRATULATIONS

You have made your way through the heart of this book and are now well informed on the problems and techniques of dollhouse construction. From this point on, as we briefly discuss two rather difficult projects, you will find that we frequently refer to the material in this chapter.

4
HIGH-RISE

Here is a miniature apartment building, complete with lobby, elevator, and penthouse. Although our version has only five stories plus the penthouse, you can make yours taller by extending the height of the shell 9½ inches for each additional story.

On each floor there are two apartments, each with the same basic floor plan, (see Figure 68). The fun of an apartment house is in the furnishing of each apartment for a different occupant and life style. One apartment might be furnished for a pair of career girls, another for a married couple with a child, another for a portrait painter who uses his living room for a studio. A wealthy playboy might live in the penthouse, or a gangster, or an eccentric heiress who collects antiques. It takes all kinds.

For this project, many construction details will be left to your discretion and experience, with frequent reference to instructions in the previous chapter on the Colonial. Full details will be given, however, for construction and installation of the elevator and the plate-glass windows.

MATERIALS

You will need two 4-x-8-foot sheets of ½-inch plywood and two 4-x-8-foot sheets of ¼-inch plywood (see Index under

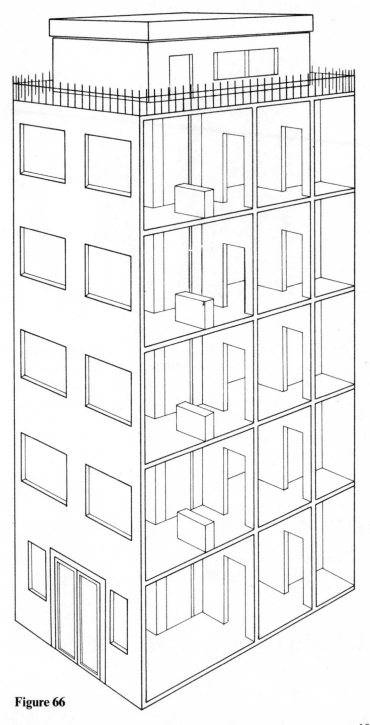

Figure 66

Figure 67

Plywood, choosing). The amount and kind of lumber required for windows, doors, woodwork, and finishing will depend on your decision as to how elaborate you intend to make the building. But the types of materials will be similar to those used for the Colonial, page 45. The special materials required are braided venetian blind cord, pulleys and counterweights for the elevator, and metal moldings and sheet acrylite for the plate-glass windows.

TOOLS

The apartment house can be built with the same tools used for the Colonial, see page 47.

CUTTING PARTS FOR THE SHELL

Cut the end walls and floors from ½-inch plywood, following the patterns shown in Figures 69 and 70.

FIRST FLOOR

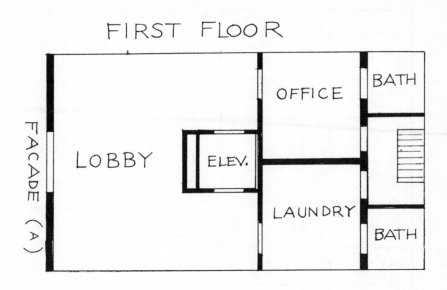

APARTMENT FLOORS

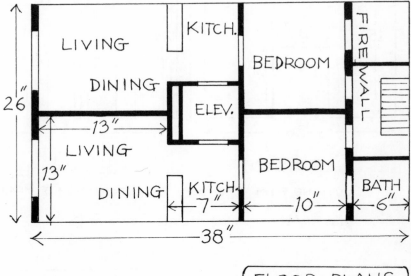

FLOOR PLANS
HIGH-RISE

Figure 68

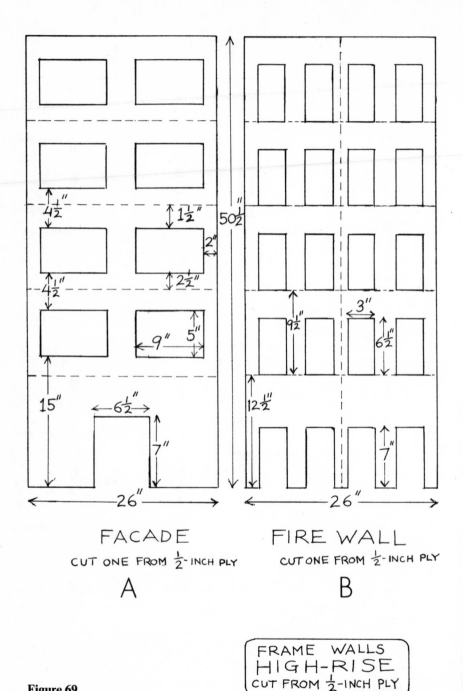

FACADE

CUT ONE FROM ½-INCH PLY

A

FIRE WALL

CUT ONE FROM ½-INCH PLY

B

FRAME WALLS
HIGH-RISE
CUT FROM ½-INCH PLY

Figure 69

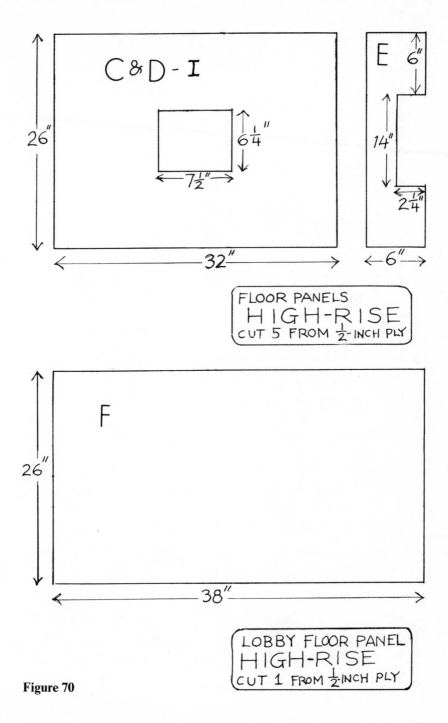

C & D - I

26"

6 1/4 "

7 1/2"

32"

E

6"

14"

2 1/4"

6"

FLOOR PANELS
HIGH-RISE
CUT 5 FROM 1/2-INCH PLY

F

26"

38"

LOBBY FLOOR PANEL
HIGH-RISE
CUT 1 FROM 1/2-INCH PLY

Figure 70

109

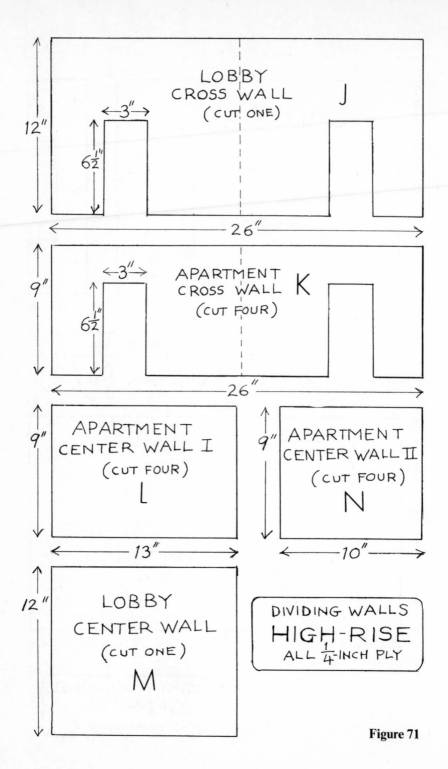

LOBBY
CROSS WALL
(CUT ONE)

J

12″

←3″→

6½″

←——————— 26″ ———————→

APARTMENT
CROSS WALL
(CUT FOUR)

K

9″

←3″→

6½″

←——————— 26″ ———————→

APARTMENT
CENTER WALL I
(CUT FOUR)

L

9″

←————— 13″ —————→

APARTMENT
CENTER WALL II
(CUT FOUR)

N

9″

←——— 10″ ———→

LOBBY
CENTER WALL
(CUT ONE)

M

12″

DIVIDING WALLS
HIGH-RISE
ALL ¼-INCH PLY

Figure 71

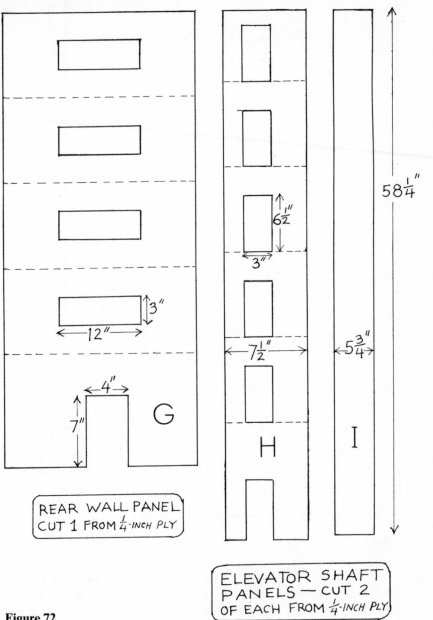

3"

12"

4"

7"

G

REAR WALL PANEL
CUT 1 FROM $\frac{1}{4}$-INCH PLY

$6\frac{1}{2}$"

3"

$7\frac{1}{2}$"

H

$5\frac{3}{4}$"

I

$58\frac{1}{4}$"

ELEVATOR SHAFT
PANELS — CUT 2
OF EACH FROM $\frac{1}{4}$-INCH PLY

Figure 72

111

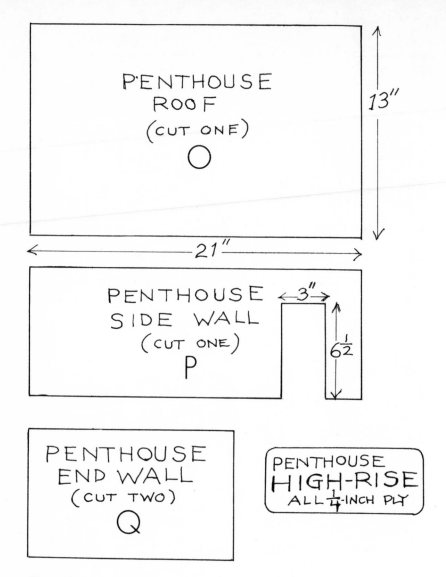

Figure 73

Cut the dividing walls, elevator shaft panels, roof panels, and penthouse walls from ¼-inch plywood, as shown in Figures 71, 72, and 73. Consult the lobby floor plan, Figure 68, first floor, for the layout of the first-floor dividing walls. For the first-floor layout you need only one cross wall and one center wall. For the apartment floors you need one cross wall and two dividing walls. Notice that the first floor (lobby) is 12 inches high, while the apartment stories are each 9 inches high.

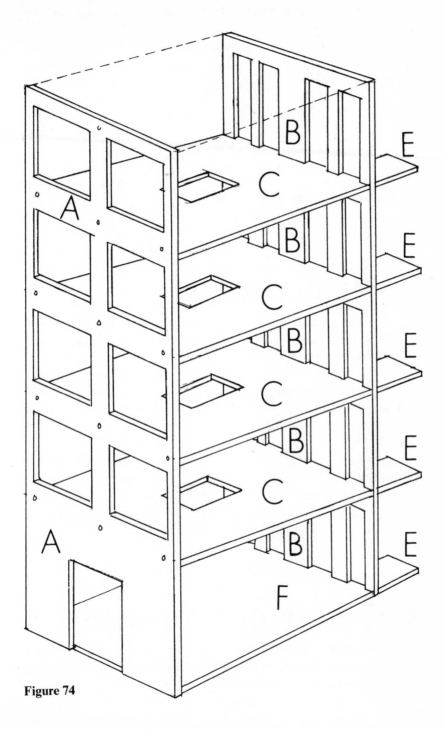

Figure 74

113

If you plan to rout grooves in the floors and ceilings to take cross-wall dividers J and K, each wall should be cut ¼ inch higher than shown in the diagrams. Once the floor panels, Figure 70, have been cut, the routing should be done.

Assemble the parts loosely, tacking them with nails. Figure 74 shows the main frame of ½-inch parts assembled, without the ¼-inch parts. To make absolutely sure your cuts are all correct, tack on the ¼-inch parts as well.

Then disassemble. Do not permanently assemble the shell until you have completed the following interior finishes: electrical wiring, wall and floor coverings, doors and windows, stairways, fireplaces (if any), elevator, and interior woodwork.

ELECTRICAL WIRING

You must decide if you are going to wire for display or if you wish to install a more complete electric system. See page 59 for a limited display system. Complete wiring for a five-story apartment house will require two or more transformers and more extensive wiring instructions than we have room for here. For help with such a system, consult your local electrician or a good dollhouse store, or write to Ed Leonard of Illinois Hobbycraft (see Appendix).

Wires that will traverse walls should be glued in place before the wall covering is glued on (see page 59). Wires that will cross floors should be buried in routed grooves before the flooring is laid (see page 63). If possible, install the transformer and fuse system before assembling the shell (see page 82).

WALL AND FLOOR COVERING

An apartment house offers an opportunity to use a variety of wall coverings. Consult the Index under Wall coverings. For flooring possibilities, see the Index under Flooring. Hardwood flooring would be suitable for the lobby, but even more striking would be stone, brick, or slate, or one of the various kinds of tiles available: glass, ceramic, or small tiles cut from real asphalt or vinyl floor tiles.

The lobby might feature an elaborate fireplace, mirrored walls, fancy wallpaper, or painted murals. There is room for statuary and even a small pond and fountain. The rear rooms behind the elevator are for maintenance offices and storage and laundry rooms; they can be decorated accordingly.

The walls and floors of the apartments can be decorated variously, depending on the tastes of their imagined occupants.

DOORS AND WINDOWS

Design of the main door depends on the overall architectural style of the building. The high-rise in Figure 66 has a modern "functional" entrance. In Figure 75 we suggest a more elaborate doorway, which might be called "art deco Gothic." But the main entrance could also be Gothic, Georgian, or pseudo-Colonial.

Figure 75

Inside doorways can be standard multi-panel (Figure 44) or solid panel (Figure 20). Consult the Index under Windows.

The large plate-glass windows at the front of the building, one to each living room, must be specially built for this project. Their frames can be made from wood or from aluminum glazing strips, available at most building supply outlets in a wide range of shapes and sizes. Figure 76 shows a window assembly of aluminum parts. The aluminum glazing strips are mitered at the corners with a hack saw and bolted or soldered in place. The window panes can be made of micro-glass or clear plastic (lucite, Perma Glaze II, or other), from 1/16 to ⅛ inch thick. Plastic can be cut with a power saw, with a heated knife blade, or with X-acto's hot knife, specially designed for the purpose.

Or you can make a wooden frame and paint it with aluminum paint. Cut the frame parts from basswood or pine in the dimensions suggested in Figure 76. Correct any errors; then sand and glue the main frame together, B. Cut the pane, C, from micro-glass or plastic and glue it into the frame, B. Then add the glazing frame, D, to finish.

Allow the pieces to dry, sand them, and paint them with aluminum paint.

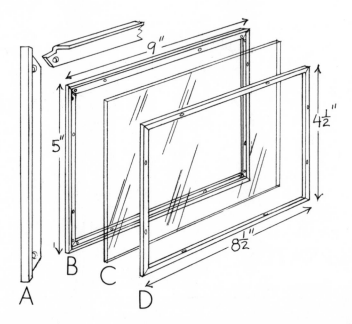

Figure 76

Install and finish the windows inside and out. See Index under Windows.

STAIRWAYS

The rear stairway is in an enclosed stairwell, as shown in Figure 77. We have cut open air ports in the fire wall, G, Figure 72. Consult the Index under Stairways for construction details. This stairway may be built with almost any kind of wood. Rather than assemble the stairs from stringers, risers, and treads, you might elect to saw each stair length from a solid chunk of 2-x-4-inch pine or fir, as suggested in Figure 24.

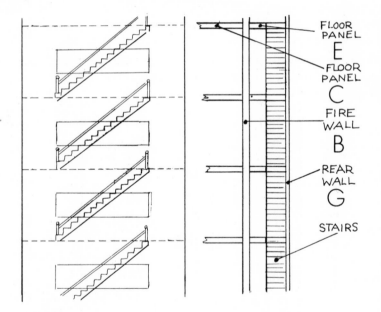

FLOOR
PANEL

E

FLOOR
PANEL

C

FIRE
WALL

B

REAR
WALL

G

STAIRS

Figure 77

ELEVATOR

The elevator car and its machinery—R, T, V, and W—are built separately from the shaft and installed while the whole shell is being assembled. But the vertical guide rail, S, must be glued to the shaft wall before the shell is assembled. Once the entire

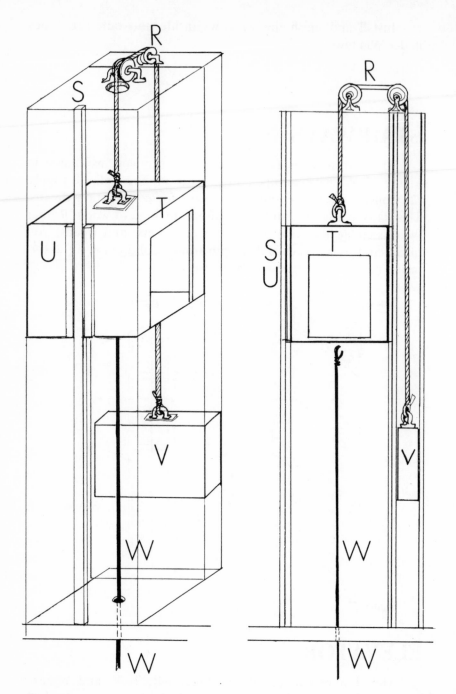

Figure 78

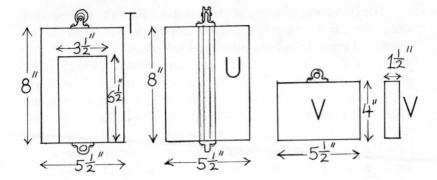

Figure 79

apparatus is installed, the elevator car will travel up and down the vertical rails, S, on each side of the shaft. The counterweight, V, slides up and down in a separate compartment of the shaft.

The car rails are cut from ½-x-½-inch pine or basswood in a length equal to the distance from the bottom of the base of the shaft to the topmost point of the elevator car within the penthouse on the roof (see Figure 80). If your lengths of ½-inch rail are not long enough, you will have to extend them with added lengths. Butt-end the ends of the strips firmly to make a smooth join. Sand the joints until they are smooth, and "grease" the rails with soap or beeswax.

The elevator car is made from ¼-inch plywood in the dimensions shown in Figure 79. The car has two doors located on opposite walls. These are left open, and as the elevator arrives at each floor, they will align with the doors in the shaft, H, Figure 72. The shaft doorways can be equipped with sliding slab doors. Such doors should be mounted on the shaft openings before the shell is assembled.

Note that the car has a double line of ½-inch strips on the opposite outside walls. These serve as outside guides to keep the car against the shaft guide wall. They should be positioned slightly more than ½ inch apart so that they can hug the guide rail, but if they fit too snugly, the car will jam.

The rise-descend mechanism, R, Figure 78, consists of a set of one or more cords, or cables, attached to the top of the car and running up to the top of the shaft, over a pulley, and down to the counterweight. In addition, there is another cord, or wire, W, attached to the bottom of the car and running down through the bottom of the shaft and out to the side of the apartment house.

The counterweights are slightly heavier than the car, so that when the car is empty, the counterweights will tend to go downward toward the bottom of the shaft, draw on the cord that goes over the pulley, and pull the car upward. However, by pulling on the other cord, W, you can draw the car downward, while the counterweight rises in its separate shaft compartment. Easing the tension on the draw cord, W, allows the car to rise; pulling it draws the car down; holding the draw cord at any point halts the car. The push-pull balance between the draw cord and the counterweight assures a steady rise and fall of the car and smooth stops at each floor.

Fixed pulleys, such as those shown, R, Figure 78, are available in some hardware stores and marine supply outlets. They are bolted to a ¼-inch plywood panel, which will be positioned at the top of the shaft. For the cable, try to get braided cording of the sort used to open and close venetian blinds. It is less likely to kink and snarl the pulley. Make the downward draw cord, W, of the same material.

If you have an erector-set motor or other small electric motor, you can operate the elevator with electric power. Omit the downward draw cord and move the main cable by direct power. This can be applied to the pulley by means a direct drive shaft. This is a difficult mechanical project, but you can get help from the plans offered in the larger erector sets.

The counterweight can be a small box of thin aluminum or ¼-inch ply, in the dimensions shown, V, Figure 79, with the sling connection on top for attaching the cable. Fill the box with earth weighing an ounce or more than the car. When temporarily assembling the shaft and testing the rise-descend mechanism, try to achieve the exact weight balance between the counterweight and the car. There should be just enough extra weight in the counterweight to draw it slowly downward, while the car proceeds upward to the top of the shaft.

Instead of a box, you can use real counterweights made from lead or clay or from steel scraps hung on a carriage of vertical rods.

Once the elevator components are ready, loosely assemble the shaft by holding it together with tape or rubber bands. Try the car for fit, and the lift mechanism for smoothness of operation. Then disassemble both the shaft and the mechanism and lay them aside until you assemble the shell.

THE ROOF

The penthouse parts are cut from ¼-inch ply, as shown in Figure 73. In addition to the penthouse, the roof could feature a small water tower. The terrace railing, indicated at the top of Figure 80, can be made from various materials. Consult the Index under Stair rail. The penthouse roof can be coated with tar or painted with black matte latex or acrylic.

ASSEMBLING THE SHELL

Use the same general procedure for assembling the shell as you used for the Colonial (page 79). You will need at least one other person to help you hold the pieces in position while you glue and nail. First, assemble the ½-inch plywood pieces into the basic frame shown in Figure 74. Glue them with white glue or contact cement. Then nail them together with 1-inch wire nails, or, better yet, drill and set 1-inch screws at crucial points. Notice that the rear floor pieces, D in Figure 70 and Figure 74, are separate from the main-floor pieces, C, and must be butted into the fire wall, B. Prop them in place until the glue dries by supporting them with a nailed strip, or with the rear wall panel itself, G, Figure 72.

Once the basic frame of ½-inch ply pieces is assembled, hook the wiring components together. Then assemble and install the elevator shaft and machinery.

Next, glue and nail the dividing walls in place, according to Figures 66 and 80. The letters in Figure 80 provide cross references to Figures 69 through 74.

Glue the lengths of stairway into position against the fire wall, zigzagging them from floor to floor, as indicated in Figure 77. When the stairs are in place, glue and nail the rear wall panel, G, Figure 72.

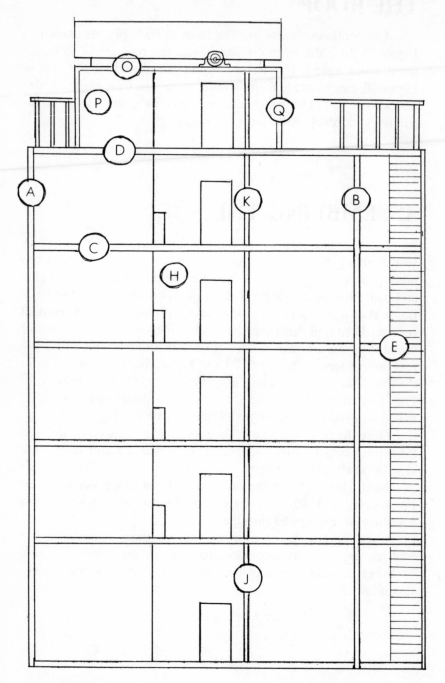

Figure 80

INSTALLING THE ELEVATOR

First, lower the counterweight into its part of the shaft, and the car into the other. See that the lift cord runs over the pulley, and that the pulley and platform are lowered onto the top of the shaft and glued in position. Push the draw-down cord through the hole in the bottom of the shaft and out through the side of the building. Once you are confident the mechanism works, glue down the top of the elevator shaft.

Now you can assemble the penthouse and glue it into position on the roof.

Finally, complete the interior details of wiring, woodwork, etc.

FINISHING THE OUTSIDE OF THE SHELL

The outer wall surfaces can be finished to resemble stone, brick, plaster, or clapboard. Brick is the most commonly used surface for an apartment house of this size. Consult the Index under Siding, Brick, Stone, and Clapboard effects.

Paint the woodwork, window frames, and door frames the color of your choice. Paint the rear stairwell and stairs in a suitable color, such as battleship gray or off-white.

5
VICTORIAN

Here are plans and notes for the construction of an eight-room Victorian mansion. The basic building can be converted into a fairy-tale palace by making a few changes in the exterior profile, according to the suggestions given at the end of this chapter.

The Victorian mansion and its variations are very ambitious projects. Each will require six months or more of part-time work. Many of the required materials, tools, and techniques have already been described in the chapter on the Colonial. This chapter, therefore, consists mainly of dimensional diagrams and general suggestions, with numerous cross references to information elsewhere in the book. We are presuming that anyone who undertakes this project has the skill and ingenuity required to finish it without intricately detailed instructions.

MATERIALS

You will need three 4-x-8-foot sheets of ½-inch plywood and four 4-x-8-foot sheets of ¼-inch plywood. See Index for help in choosing plywood. The required types of small lumber and other materials will be similar to those used for the Colonial, page 45. The only materials unique to this dollhouse are the newels and

Figure 81

other millwork used for decorating the porch, balcony, and eaves—distinguishing features of Victorian architecture. See the Appendix for sources of such decorative "gingerbread."

TOOLS

The Victorian can be built with the same tools used for the Colonial, page 47.

Figure 82

CUTTING PARTS FOR THE SHELL

First examine the floor plans in Figures 83 and 84 to get an idea of the layout. Then cut the three floor panels shown in Figure 85 and the two end panels from ½-inch plywood, as shown in D and E, Figure 86. Note the two stairwell notches in panel B, the one stairwell notch in the attic-floor panel C, and the long slot in the first-floor panel A. The slot is ½ inch wide. The end wall, D, will be slipped into the slot when the shell is assembled.

Cut the rest of the shell parts out of ¼-inch plywood, as shown in Figures 86 through 92. When more than one piece of

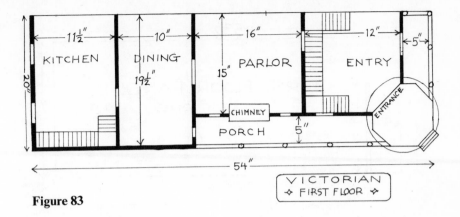

Figure 83

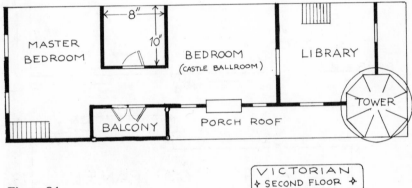

Figure 84

any part is required, the number of copies is indicated, for example: Tower Panel U, Figure 91, cut five.

The circular porch roof, called the tower base, X, Figure 91, is cut from a 1-inch slab of pine or fir in the shape and dimensions shown.

Once all the parts have been cut, temporarily assemble the shell. Hold the parts in place with masking tape or tack them together with small nails. Check your assembly against Figures 89, 92, and 93 to be sure you have all the needed parts and that they fit correctly.

Disassemble the shell before you complete the interior finish: electrical wiring, wall and floor coverings, doors and windows, stairways, fireplaces, and interior woodwork. If you need information about any of these categories, consult the Index.

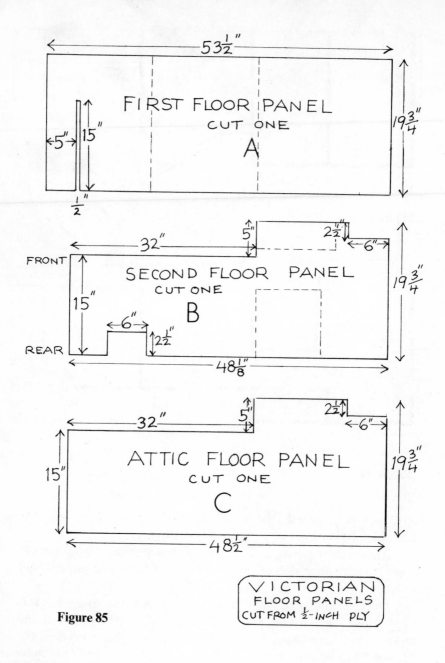

Figure 85

VICTORIAN
FLOOR PANELS
CUT FROM ½-INCH PLY

ELECTRICAL WIRING

See page 59 for installation of a limited electrical system designed for display. For a realistic effect, a Victorian house

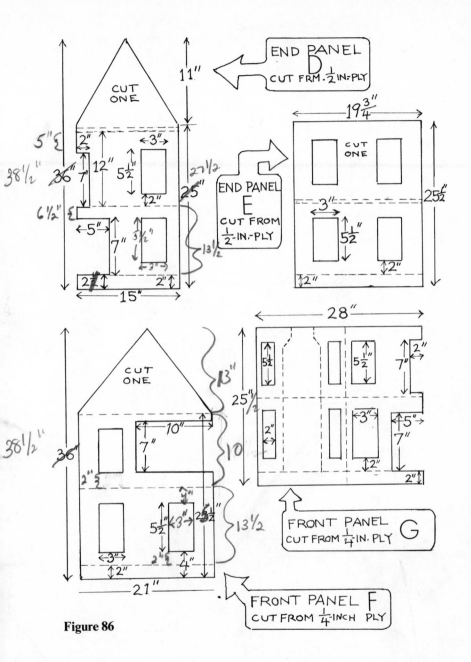

Figure 86

should feature overhead lighting, including chandeliers in the downstairs entrance hall and in the upstairs library. For help with such a system, consult your local electrician, or a good dollhouse store, or write to Ed Leonard, listed in the Appendix.

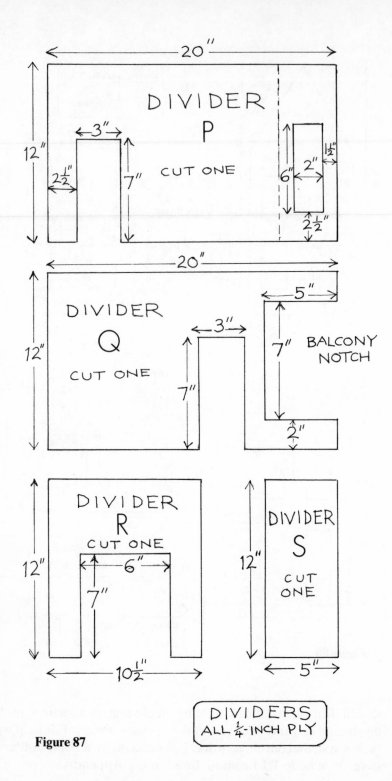

Figure 87

Wires that traverse walls should be glued in place before the wall covering is applied (see Figure 39). Wires that cross floors should be buried in routed grooves before the flooring is installed. The transformer and fuse holder can be installed in the attic and attached to Floor Panel C, Figure 85, before the shell is assembled.

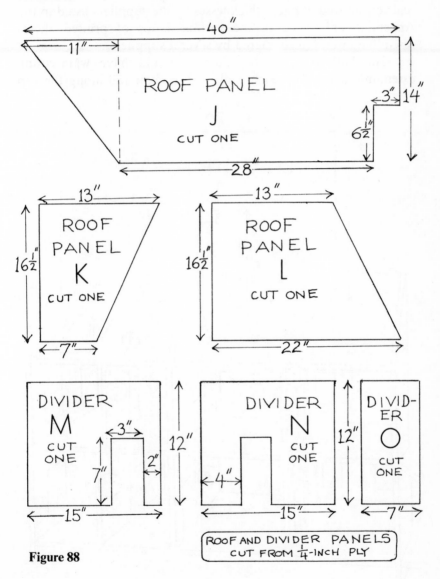

Figure 88

WALL AND FLOOR COVERINGS

Victorian houses usually have wallpaper in most of the rooms. Use small-figured fabric (see page 61), or order authentic miniature Victorian wallpapers from the suppliers listed in the Appendix. The library or study might be paneled in wood—either real veneer, sold in micro-thicknesses by the suppliers listed in the Appendix, or in one of the various kinds of printed sheets resembling wood (also offered by several suppliers).

The hallways and the kitchen should have wainscoting extending halfway up each wall, with a chair rail along the top

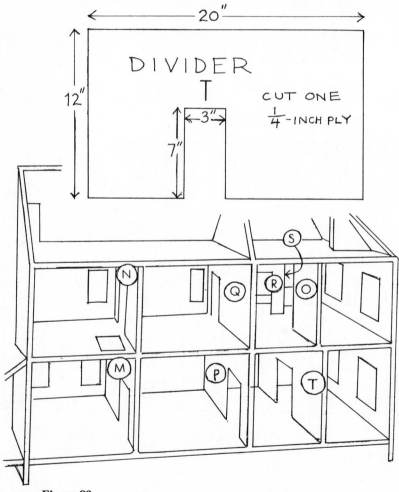

Figure 89

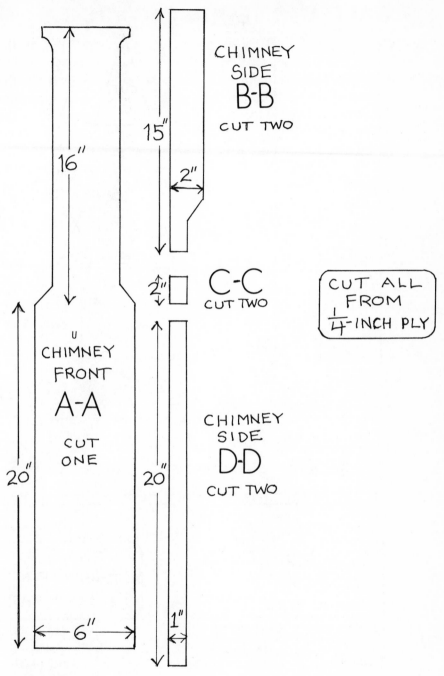

CHIMNEY
SIDE
B-B

CUT TWO

15"

2"

CUT ALL
FROM
$\frac{1}{4}$-INCH PLY

C-C
CUT TWO

2"

16"

ᴜ CHIMNEY
FRONT
A-A

CUT
ONE

CHIMNEY
SIDE
D-D

CUT TWO

20"

20"

6"

1"

Figure 90

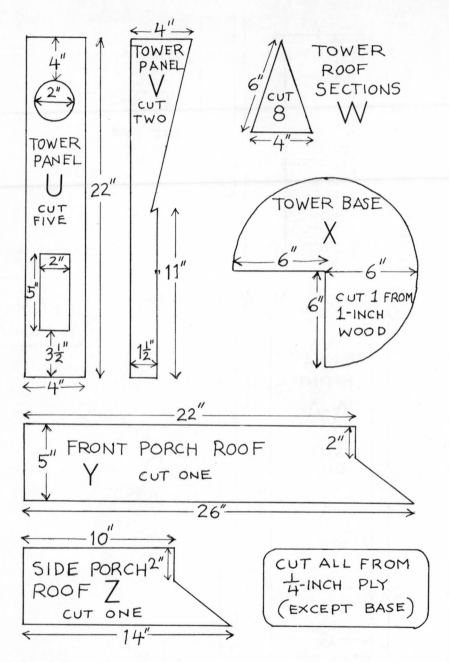

4"

TOWER
PANEL
V
CUT
TWO

4"

TOWER
PANEL
U

CUT
FIVE

22"

11"

1½"

5"

2"

3½"

4"

6"

CUT
8

4"

TOWER
ROOF
SECTIONS
W

TOWER BASE
X

6"

6"

6"

CUT 1 FROM
1-INCH
WOOD

22"

FRONT PORCH ROOF
Y   CUT ONE

5"

2"

26"

10"

SIDE PORCH ROOF Z

CUT ONE

2"

14"

CUT ALL FROM
¼-INCH PLY
(EXCEPT BASE)

Figure 91

edge at the height of the back of a miniature chair. The dining room might have a plate ledge made from one of the various moldings offered by the suppliers listed in our Appendix. Consult the Index for other wall-covering possibilities and instructions.

For various flooring materials, consult pages 33–34 and the Index. The floors of Victorian houses are usually hardwood, sometimes parquet. If you plan to build the Titania's Palace conversion, suggested at the end of this chapter, you may choose to pave your floors with any number of exotic coverings, such as stone, brick, or tile. Consult the Index under those headings and under Flooring. See the Appendix for the list of suppliers. You may even decide to cover the walls of at least one Palace room entirely with mirrors.

DOORS AND WINDOWS

Victorian doors and windows are generally taller than their modern counterparts. Windows are most often multi-paned, either six over six or eight over eight (see Figure 10). Doors are usually of the six-panel type and can be made from scratch, put together from kits (see Figure 44), or purchased already assembled. Consult the Index under Doors.

The windows in the tower of your Victorian can be glazed with colored plastic or micro-glass. You might even choose to make simulated stained-glass windows by gluing shapes of colored plastic onto a base sheet of clear lucite or other plastic sheeting.

STAIRWAYS

This Victorian has two stairways, one at the front of the house, going from the first floor to the second, and the other at the rear of the house, leading from the kitchen all the way to the attic. The front stairway should be finely finished with hardwood treads and handrails; the rear stairway can be relatively simple. See the Index under Stairways, and page 35.

135

FIREPLACES

Victorian fireplaces can be simple or elaborate; many authentic Victorian houses have fireplaces in the bedrooms as well as in the parlor or living room. Various kinds of fireplaces are available through the suppliers listed in the Appendix. See Index under Fireplaces.

INTERIOR WOODWORK

As mentioned previously, wainscoting and chair rails are common features of Victorian interior woodwork. They are often stained and then finished with a clear varnish. If you intend to have such a finish for any woodwork, take great care during assembly to avoid bulges and smears of glue, since they will show through any stain or varnish.

Once all or most of the interior details are in place, the shell can be assembled.

ASSEMBLING THE SHELL

Study the floor plans in Figures 83 and 84. Assemble parts A, B, C, D, E, and F into the basic frame shown at the top of Figure 92. Glue the parts with contact cement or epoxy, then further secure them with 1-inch wire nails or 1-inch flatheaded screws. Use shorter nails or screws for the ¼-inch piece, F.

Next, add the ¼-inch front panel, G, as shown in Figure 93.

Glue the two triangular attic dividers, H and I, upright on the attic floor, as shown in Figure 92. These will help support the roof panels.

Next, add the three front roof panels—J, K, and L—as shown in Figure 93. You may also want to add a set of rear roof panels. Cut them to fit and hinge them, as suggested in Figure 58.

From a slab of 1-inch pine or fir cut and position the circular

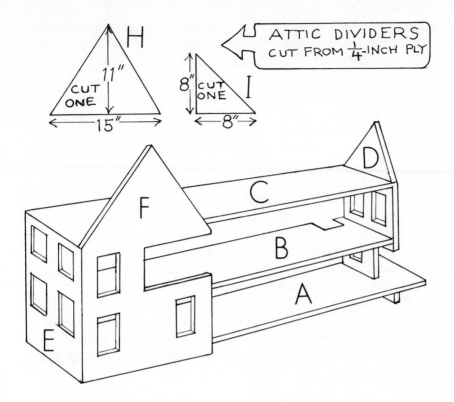

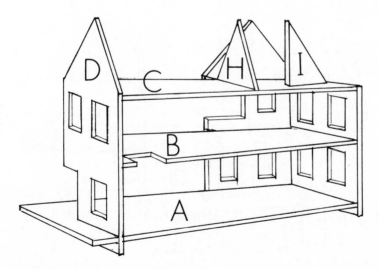

Figure 92

porch roof, called tower base, X, Figure 91. Sand their top and bottom edges to give them somewhat the contour of a doughnut. Then glue them into position, as shown, X, in Figure 93.

To put the tower together, glue the five ¼-inch tower panels, U, Figure 91, and the two narrower tower panels, V, to form the octagonal cylinder shown, U, V, Figure 93. The tower is based on an octagonal circumference, but it is not actually a full octagon because the corner of the house eliminates one and a half side panels.

Once the tubular form is ready, assemble the eight roof sections, W, Figure 91, to form the peaked roof. Glue them in place on top of the tower. Finally, glue the tower into position atop the tower base 1-inch disk, snug around the corner of the house, as indicated in Figures 81 and 93. You will have to do a little more carpentry to complete the top rear of the tower so that it conforms to the roof slope.

Next, glue in the dividing walls, following the floor plan, Figures 83 and 84, and the diagram at the bottom of Figure 89. Note that Q extends to form part of the second-floor balcony. S and R enclose the balcony. Downstairs, divider P extends to the

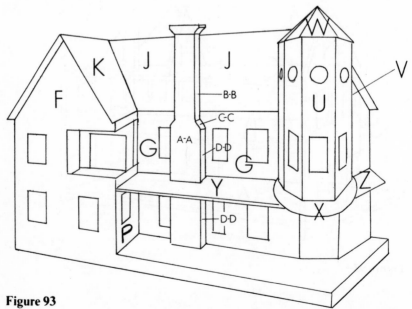

Figure 93

front of the left wing below the balcony and provides the second narrow window to the left of the chimney, Figure 93.

Assemble the chimney parts shown in Figure 90. For help in assembling the chimney, see Figure 59 and consult page 94 of the text.

Next, add the two porch roofs, Y and Z, as shown in Figure 93.

Narrow, 2-inch-wide foundation panels of ¼-inch ply can now be added around the base of the porch.

FINISHING THE OUTSIDE

The outside walls can be painted solid, or painted with lines to imitate clapboard siding (see page 12). Victorian houses are most often finished on the outside with clapboard siding, which can be made from scratch (see Figure 61), or they can be purchased from the suppliers listed in the Appendix. Consult the Index for Stone or Brick effects.

The roof can be painted solid, also, or painted with a shingle effect. Or it can be covered with miniature shingles, either pseudo-asphalt, Figure 26, or cedar, Figure 60. Consult the Index under Shingles.

The chimney can be painted red. It can also be painted with a brick effect, or covered with one of the three-dimensional brick or stone materials. You have similar choices for finishing the porch foundation. See Index under Stone and Brick effects.

The balustrades of the front porch and the corner balcony can be as elaborate as you choose. Intricately turned newels of various shapes and sizes are available in dollhouse shops and through the suppliers listed in the Appendix. Similar fine woodwork is available for the gingerbread work on the upper balcony and for the roof peak, as suggested in Figure 81.

You can add even more gingerbread woodwork than we have suggested. Victorian houses often have complicated beading along the roof eaves. Fancy woodwork strips are available at your local lumber outlet. They are often too large for dollhouse work, but some of them can be cut in half lengthwise. They provide effective scrollwork, beading, and rope patterns.

Painting a Victorian can be fun, for the many angles and fancy woodwork provide convenient divisions for two-tone effects. You might paint the side walls a light gray and the woodwork of the windows, doors, and eaves a dark iron gray. Or try other combinations of color: beige and black, brown and yellow, light blue and indigo. Some Victorian houses are painted in as many as three or four colors.

FURNISHING

Furnishing a Victorian is not difficult, since a great deal of the miniature furniture available is copied from turn-of-the-century models. But always be cautious before buying any furniture and make comparisons whenever possible, for the matter of comparative scale is a touchy business. Sometimes a piece that is mathematically in scale will seem too large or too

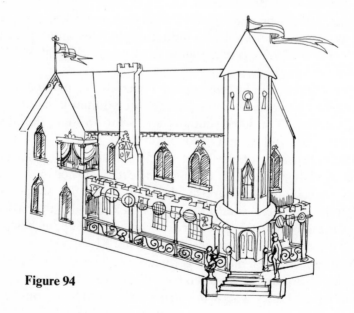

Figure 94

small in your particular setting. It helps to take along one or two pieces of your present furniture for comparison purposes when you buy new furniture.

ALTERNATIVE USE

Some of the most famous dollhouses of history have been miniature palaces. Major Sir Nevile Wilkinson, builder of the famous Titania's Palace, claimed that he received instructions for the dollhouse directly from a fairy named Titania.

The basic shell of our Victorian house can be converted into a fairy-tale palace or a replica of a medieval crusader's palace. We offer some conversion suggestions in Figure 94. The interior of a palace might be very ornate, with glass chandeliers in most of the rooms, elaborate tiled floors, and mirrored walls.

APPENDIX

BOOKS AND MAGAZINES

Books:

Downing, A. J. *The Architecture of Country Houses*. New York: Dover, 1969.

Farlie, Barbara L., and Clark, Charlotte L. *All About Doll Houses*. New York: Crown, 1975.

Gillon, Edmund V., Jr., and Lancaster, Clay. *Victorian Houses: A Treasure of Lesser-Known Examples*. New York: Dover, 1973.

Jacobs, Flora Gill. *Dolls' Houses in America*. New York: Charles Scribner's Sons, 1974.

Kelly, J. Frederick. *Early Domestic Architecture of Connecticut*. New York: Dover, 1952.

O'Brien, Marian M. *Make Your Own Dollhouses and Dollhouse Miniatures*. New York: Hawthorne Books, 1975.

Rosner, Bernard, and Beckerman, Jay. *Inside the World of Miniatures and Dollhouses*. New York: David McKay, 1976.

Magazines

Miniature Gazette. Published quarterly and sent to all members of the National Association of Miniature Enthusiasts. To apply for membership, query the Association, care of Box 2621, Brookhurst Center, Anaheim, California 92804.

Nutshell News. Edited by Catherine B. MacLaren. 1035 Newkirk Drive, La Jolla, California 92037.

A.I.M.M. Mott Miniature Workshop News. Detailed instructions for miniature projects, published once a year. Box 5514, Sunny Hills Station, Fullerton, California 92635.

Creative Crafts. Editor, Sybil Harp. Crafts in general, but up to a third devoted to miniatures. Bimonthly. Circulation Manager, *Creative Crafts,* P.O. Box 700, Newton, New Jersey 07860.

SUPPLIERS

A & L Hobbicraft
50 Broadway, Box 7025
Asheville, N.C. 28802

Tiles of all kinds.

P. S. Andrews Co.
603 So. Main Street
St. Charles, Mo. 63301

Tools and supplies.

Architectural Model Supplies, Inc.
115D Bellam Boulevard
P.O. Box 3497
San Rafael, Calif. 94942

Trees, grass, basswood, paints, surface materials.

American Edelstaal, Inc.
1 Atwood Avenue
Tenafly, N. J. 07670

Unimat miniature machine tool. Also sold in hardware stores.

Bob's Arts and Crafts
11880 No. Washington
Northglenn, Colo. 80233

All supplies.

C. E. Bergeron
123 Laurel Avenue
Bradford, Mass. 01830

All varieties of molding and woodwork.

Brown's Miniatures
P.O. Box 35
Cambridge, N. Y. 12816

Metal miniature accessories.

Chestnut Hill Studio
12 Woodcreek Drive
Taylors, S. C. 29687

Doors, windows, and paneling, plus furniture and other accessories.

Clare-Bell Brassworks
Queen Street
Southington, Conn. 06489

Precision brass miniatures.

Constantine's
2050 Eastchester Road
Bronx, N.Y. 10461

Tools, hardware, woods to 1/16 inch, veneers to 1/28 inch.

Craft Creative Kits
Elmhurst, Ill. 60126

Doors, windows, and houses.

Craftsman Wood Service
Company
2727 South Mary Street
Chicago, Ill. 60608

Tools, hardware, wood in all sizes.

Dollhouse Factory
Box 456, 156 Main Street
Lebanon, N.J. 08833

Hand-made cedar shingles, leaded
windows, light fixtures.

Dollhouses
16460 Wagon Wheel Drive
Riverside, Calif. 92506

Glass, mirrors, accessories.

Dremel Manufacturing Division
Emerson Electric Co.
4915 21st Street
Racine, Wisc. 53406

Power tools. Also available in
hardware stores and dollhouse
shops.

Edabub's Dollhouse
R.D. 1, Box 84 B
Great Barrington, Mass. 01230

Clapboard siding, flooring, wainscoting, moldings.

Enchanted Toy Shop Dept. DHN
23812 Lorain Road
No. Olmstead, Ohio 44070

Electric wiring and accessories.

The Ginger Jar
6133 Wakefield Drive
Sylvania, Ohio 43560

Bricks, other accessories.

Granny's Attic
381 Rockaway Avenue
Valley Stream, N.Y. 11581

Retail outlet that also manufac-
tures clapboard siding in sheets.
Informed and helpful staff, one of
many such retail stores. See your
local yellow pages under Crafts,
Dollhouses.

J. Hermes
Box 23
El Monte Calif. 91734

Wallpapers and glues.

Holgate & Reynolds
601 Davis Street
Evanston, Ill. 60201

Brick, stone, and other scale-model
plastic surfaces.

Illinois Hobbycraft (Ed Leonard)
12 So. Fifth Street
Geneva, Ill. 60134

Lighting equipment; manufacturer, retailer, and wholesaler.
Excellent wiring instruction sheets.

Metal Miniatures
601 Davis Street
Evanston, Ill. 60201

Fine door knobs, castings,
wallpapers.

Northeastern Scale Models Inc.
Box 425

144

Methuen, Mass. 01844

Manufacturer of miniature lumber of all kinds, moldings, doors and doorways, windows that go up and down.

Posy Patch Originals
P.O. Box 38123
Atlanta, Ga. 30334

Miniature flowers and plants.

Doreen Sinnett Designs
418 Santa Ana Avenue
Newport Beach, Calif. 92660

Wallpapers, brick effects, shingles, and other materials

The Village Smithy
R.D. 5, Hemlock Trail
Carmel, New York 10512

Wrought iron and other metal hardware and accessories.

The Workshop
424 No. Broadview
Wichita, Kan. 67208

Fireplaces, excellent doors and windows, flooring and molding.

COMMON METRIC EQUIVALENTS
AND CONVERSIONS

Approximate

1 inch	= 25 millimeters
1 foot	= 0.3 meter
1 yard	= 0.9 meter
1 square inch	= 6.5 square centimeters
1 square foot	= 0.09 square meter
1 square yard	= 0.8 square meter
1 millimeter	= 0.04 inch
1 meter	= 3.3 feet
1 meter	= 1.1 yards
1 square centimeter	= 0.16 square inch

Accurate to Parts Per Million

inches × 25.4	= millimeters
feet × 0.3048	= meters
yards × 0.9144	= meters
square inches × 6.4516	= square centimeters
square feet × 0.092903	= square meters
square yards × 0.836127	= square meters

INDEX